Ultimate Presentations

Jay Surti

U|timate
Presentations

Master the art of giving
fantastic presentations
and wowing employers

KoganPage

First published in Great Britain and the United States in 2018 by Kogan Page Limited

2nd Floor, 45 Gee Street	c/o Martin P Hill Consulting	4737/23 Ansari Road
London	122 W 27th Street	Daryaganj
EC1V 3RS	New York, NY 10001	New Delhi 110002
United Kingdom	USA	India

© Jay Surti 2018

ISBN   978 0 7494 8130 8
E-ISBN   978 0 7494 8131 5

British Library Cataloguing-in-Publication Data

A CIP record for this book is available from the British Library.

Typeset by Integra Software Services, Pondicherry
Print production managed by Jellyfish
Printed and bound in Great Britain by CPI Group (UK) Ltd, Croydon CR0 4YY

CONTENTS

INTRODUCTION

Presentations are a part of life in the workplace – they feature in all industries and in many different situations within those industries. Being able to master your presentation technique will help boost your career.

If you are just getting started on your career path, there are many chapters that will take you through the art of constructing your content and delivering it in a way that engages an audience, as well as showing you how to set yourself up for success when presenting at an interview or assessment centre. As you progress through your career and become more experienced, you'll meet new challenges. No matter where you are in your speaking journey, if you're looking for new improvements to take you to the next level, you'll find them in this book. I'll show you how.

The main focus of this book is based around presentations of course, but there are also many tools and tips that have wider applications in communication generally. For example we'll look at the impact of non-verbal communication and ways in which we all like to process information. This will give you the inside track on how to better understand and connect with team members, senior managers and clients. I've also included a host of tips on how to tackle difficult questions – useful not just in the context of the question and answer section of presentations but in any kind of meeting from interviews to business pitches. Each chapter is dedicated to a different topic to make it easy for you to skip straight to the one that you need. I would recommend that you look at all of the chapters even if you think you feel confident in some areas already – it's always worth refreshing what you know and perhaps you'll come across a different way of looking at something or a new tip! I therefore suggest reading through this book from beginning to end as each chapter will build upon the previous one, and give you an all-round solid grounding in presenting. However, if you have a specific area you want to brush up on right away, you can skip to the chapters you need. For example, if you have an interview coming up, you might want to go straight to Chapter 19.

I've shared plenty of examples demonstrating both good and bad techniques to give you insights as to the best way to apply them or keep improving – some of those are from my own personal experience. I was once a young professional too – one with very little presentation experience and not enough confidence. In my personal opinion, I don't think there is enough emphasis placed upon learning how to hone presentation skills in school and university and yet being able to present is a requirement in most jobs.

Over the years I've coached and worked with people of all age groups in many industries and what most of them have in common is that they lack confidence and have very little idea as to how to be engaging when speaking to groups. Some people do seem like they are naturally talented and have a knack for speaking in public, but they are just more experienced and well prepared. The good news is that anyone can learn how to be better at presenting – it just takes a little time.

Wherever you're starting from, if you're willing to put in the effort you will make a positive impression on any audience. You might even start to enjoy presenting, like I did!

1

WHY PRESENTATION SKILLS ARE IMPORTANT

Presentation skills are important in the workplace both for individual success and business success. In the competitive world that we live in, it is no longer enough just to have the necessary capability to carry out your job. You need to be able to communicate effectively as well. This means conquering your fears and learning to love speaking under pressure.

Whether you're speaking to a client on the phone, or presenting to an external audience, your presentation skills not only reflect you but also your organization. You act as a representative of your company every time you enter into an interaction with external stakeholders such as clients, suppliers or other partnership agencies. This is why employers are looking for individuals that can impress through a well-crafted and confident presentation. Honing these skills gives you the best chance of securing the career path of dreams.

A good presentation can be a very powerful way to communicate an idea or message. It is a skill that is highly valued and is one that anyone can improve upon.

Improve your personal brand

Becoming a good presenter will also raise your profile and enhance your personal brand. All too often people put too much focus upon the content and don't give enough attention to how they deliver it. It doesn't matter what career or industry sector you're in, we are all in the business of selling. Whatever roles you take on along your career path, you will need to sell an idea or concept in order to get buy in from others – colleagues, managers or clients. Whatever industry you are in or looking to find a position in, here are some of the benefits of improving presentation skills:

- You become more visible and get noticed – not many people take up the challenge of giving presentations. Those that do get more exposure by having the opportunity to get in front of people they don't see on a day to day basis sitting at their desks or within their teams.
- You are memorable – by mastering presentation skills you build a reputation for being a great communicator.
- You are able to win people over to your ideas when you know how to connect with them and can set out your arguments clearly and persuasively
- You are chosen to attend more client meetings and can become more integral to client relationships by virtue of the fact that you have a reputation for being an effective communicator.
- You come across as confident
- You develop a wider network – people get to know who you are and what you can do so will approach you more often.

All of the above can help you strengthen your career path as well as give you a strong foundation for leadership opportunities. Great leaders have great communication skills.

When we think about presentations we often conjure up images in our mind of formal speeches in front of a large group. In reality we present and influence every day through our daily interactions at work and in our personal lives. In this book, we will look at how to leverage what you already do and help you become more effective. Even if you don't have to give presentations as part of your job right now, you probably will have to in future.

In their book *The Start-up of You*, Reid Hoffman (co-founder of LinkedIn) and Ben Casnocha discuss the concept of thinking of ourselves as entrepreneurs. What they mean by that is not that we should all think about starting companies but that we should all create our own brands and take responsibility for developing ourselves. Today there is huge global competition for jobs. The traditional career pathway where employers sponsor your education is gone. There is an expectation now that you hit the ground running and can bring more to the party than your fellow applicants. You need to develop a competitive advantage and being able to communicate with your audience persuasively gives you that edge.

How fear of speaking can hold you back

Depending upon which article or research survey you read, the fear of presenting in front of others seems to be among the top three most common human fears – right alongside the fear of dying!

This might sound extreme but public speaking taps into a very real and deep-seated fear that humans share: the fear of rejection. We worry about being judged or looking silly in front of others during a presentation. It's an irrational fear but there are things we can do about it.

The physical symptoms that we associate with anxiety around public speaking include increased heart rate, faster breathing and sweating. What's happening is that there is an adrenaline rush. This is the body's way of getting ready for a fight or flight situation – to be on high alert. For our ancestors this type of response helped them to deal with being threatened by a scary beast. These situations are no longer relevant for us but our minds interpret perceived threatening situations like public speaking in the same way.

This fear can be so bad that many of us will do almost anything to avoid speaking in front of groups. I can speak from personal experience because it's what I did for years – make excuses again and again to get out of having to speak.

For most of my early life I had a debilitating fear of public speaking. I found it incredibly difficult to speak up even in small groups. Somehow I managed to carve out a career in law but still constantly avoided opportunities to present in team meetings or seminars. Ultimately though, I had to represent clients in court. The only way I could get through these presentations was to prepare extremely well but, even then, the fear would make me feel sick. After a few more years into my career I realized that my lack of presentation skills was holding me back: other people were taking opportunities that I could have had. It was clear that the only way I could get ahead was to work on the one thing that I feared the most – speaking in front of groups.

The turning point for me came when I had been asked to give a ten-minute update in a team meeting on a recent development in the law. I had been given two weeks' notice, which should have been more than enough time to prepare. However, I just kept putting it off because of nerves: I was in denial and buried my head in the sand. On the day of the presentation, I was woefully underprepared and incredibly nervous. I was unable to finish the update so a colleague had to step in and save me. I was mortified. That day I decided something like that would never happen to me again. I was determined to find a solution to my lack of confidence in speaking. What happened next was a process in which I actually started to enjoy speaking and ended up learning so much more than I expected about presentation skills, confidence and techniques.

My first action was to search the internet to look for help and I found a speaking club near my office that I could join. The advantage of this was that I could build my confidence and develop my skills outside of work without feeling embarrassed.

It took me three months to pluck up the courage to get up to the front of the room and give a mini speech at the club, but it was a start. Gradually over the next few months I started to feel a little more comfortable about getting up to speak in front of groups. However, I knew that I needed to do more to become a truly skilled presenter. I took off holiday time to attend presentation workshops and boot camps in the US. The intensity of having to write and deliver speeches multiple times within a short space of time made a huge difference to my comfort zone and my abilities. I then gradually volunteered to speak at team meetings when an update on training was required and steadily became an experienced and comfortable public speaker, with it now being a major part of my working life.

Committing to improving your skills is the most important thing and, in this book, I will give you a roadmap to do just this. Alongside your reading, find a way to get more experience wherever you can.

Some people never get to the stage of enjoying speaking but the point is, anyone can become more confident and competent if they are prepared to put some effort in. I don't believe great speakers are born. I think we all have the ability to be effective communicators, we just have to focus on honing our skills.

Taking charge and working on improving your skills in this area helps boost your confidence and prepares you for situations where you might be asked to speak at short notice eg when you have to stand in for a colleague. Having a solid foundation will help towards that. The confidence you gain from feeling comfortable in presentation settings has a knock on effect to other areas of your life.

You could be the best expert in your field but if you can't articulate your message and engage with your target audience then no one will know how good you are or what you can do. Trust me when I say that I have seen some of the country's top experts in their fields present at seminars and lose their audience because they didn't craft their message in a way that engaged their audience.

Think of all the seminars or speeches you have sat through that were tedious and went on too long. Most likely they involved a huge deck of bullet point slides. Poor presentation skills mean that leaders don't inspire teams, companies lose sales and opportunities are missed. Do you want to be that kind of speaker?

How presentation skills can help with job searching

Job interviews are a kind of presentation, one where you sell yourself by communicating the reasons why you would be the best candidate for the job as clearly and as persuasively as possible. Being able to answer unseen questions in a logical manner is necessary in a situation like that.

In addition to the interview, many recruitment processes involve delivering a presentation. This task is set to test competencies such as confidence, planning and logically structuring content.

You can prepare for each of these aspects by working on your presentation skills. If you are ambitious or interested in moving up the career ladder then presentation skills will help you.

Getting better at networking

There is a close connection between being able to deliver a successful presentation and being good at networking. Both require a level confidence and the ability to speak clearly and engagingly to others. Becoming effective at networking can give you a competitive advantage. In today's highly competitive world, developing trusted relationships with people who can help you with your career is vital to career growth.

Contacts in your network can assist you through mentoring, useful introductions and providing access to industry information or best practice.

In order to grow your network and build strong relationships you have to find places to meet people first – typically at business networking events. However, many people feel uncomfortable about going to these types of events because they aren't quite sure what to say or don't feel confident talking to strangers. It doesn't have to be this way. With proper preparation and adopting the right mindset, you can have a much better experience. Many of the suggestions in this book about developing your presentation skills are equally applicable to networking.

A key point to bear in mind is that when you meet people for the first time it's important to make a good impression and hopefully you will make a connection that is worth building upon. A typical question that often gets asked is 'What do you do?' The usual way people respond is by describing their job title, which is not very imaginative or memorable:

'I'm a lawyer/banker/marketing consultant/financial adviser...'

People don't really care about what your job title or profession is – they are more interested in what you can do to help them.

A better way is to prepare a more detailed description about how what you do helps others. This is your elevator pitch – being able to sell yourself in thirty seconds. Think of it as a mini speech in a way – one that you can hone and prepare in advance. It is also important to have a clear way of describing what you do or what you are involved in so that people get a clear understanding of how they might help you or who they can connect you to.

For example, I coach professionals in presentation skills. One way in which I could introduce myself could be:

'I help ambitious professionals become more confident and engaging presenters through one to one coaching.'

That's much more descriptive than 'I am a coach.'

EXERCISE

Have a go at drafting your own introduction by using the following framework:

'I help (work with/assist/take care of etc) clients (customers/anyone else that may be relevant to you) to (achieve/get more of/reduce/understand etc).'

That first meeting isn't going to get you a new job or win you work right away but it may lead to opportunities later if you come across as interesting enough to keep in contact with.

The tips on crafting and rehearsing a presentation to make more impact with confidence that are discussed in more detail later will help you with getting your elevator pitch right.

The benchmark for workplace presentations is actually quite low – most people don't think about the audience experience. If you only take away a few concepts from this book and put them into practice, you will be much better than most of your competition.

Presentation skills are fundamental to all workplace interactions.

TOP TIPS

- A presentation task is a common occurrence in recruitment these days – it is never too soon to start improving your skills so that you set yourself up for success when you do attend an assessment centre or interview.

- Improving your presentation skills with increase your visibility and reputation at work, helping you move on up the career ladder.

- Not many people are very good as presenting effectively – the bar is quite low so you can stand out from the crowd by taking up opportunities to present and making sure you prepare well.

- Prepare for networking events by drafting your introduction in advance – choose a phrase that that immediately helps someone who has never met you before understand exactly what area of work you are involved in.

2

GIVING PRESENTATIONS AT INTERVIEWS AND ASSESSMENT CENTRES: THE ESSENTIALS

With so many talented candidates vying for every job, you have to stand out of the crowd at interview stage. Being able to deliver a fantastic presentation is a way of achieving this.

We think of careers such as sales, marketing, public relations, and teaching as obviously needing candidates with competent presentations skills. However, the ability to speak confidently and clearly is extremely relevant to almost every professional role across all industries. That is why presentations are a growing feature of interviews and assessment centres: assessors are looking for candidates who can deliver a well-structured and persuasive presentation.

I worked with Trudie, a young paralegal who had been looking for a role as a trainee solicitor for many months. Competition for legal jobs has always been tough and it's not getting any easier. She had made several applications and reached the assessment centre stage a few times but never got any further. One of the key areas where she felt vulnerable was the presentation task. The nerves of speaking combined with the pressure of preparing an unseen presentation in a short period of time was affecting her performance.

When she asked for feedback the consistent message was that the presentation element needed to be stronger and she needed to come across as more confident and engaging. That is why she reached out to me to focus on this key skill set to increase her chances of eventually securing that training contract. This was our training plan:

- First we practised some drills of impromptu questions where she hadn't seen them beforehand so she could start to feel more comfortable at thinking on her feet. We brainstormed all the possible questions she might be asked on the day such as how she coped with challenges, what ideas she had to bring the firm up to speed with social media marketing and her opinion on recent developments in the law. This helped her construct a framework for answers she could rehearse so that even if the exact same question didn't come up on the day she had some material to work with at her fingertips.

- I encouraged her to practise creating presentations. The experience of going through drafting a speech again and again helped boost her confidence and got her into the habit of structuring content in very little time.

- I attended a live presentation she was delivering to a group so that I could give her feedback on her delivery style and content structure.

Trudie took all this on board and put in a lot of preparation for the next assessment opportunity and finally succeeded in getting that job. On that day, she was asked to give a presentation explaining how the firm could increase their visibility through social media. She later told me that all that preparation not only made her feel more confident, but allowed her to be present in the moment so she could focus on allowing her personality to shine through without worrying about remembering what to say next.

The presentation exercise in an interview situation is a chance to prove yourself. You want to be memorable – this is the opportunity to do that.

In this chapter we'll go over the key things you need to be aware of to prepare for your assessment centre or interview presentation. In later chapters we go into much more detail looking at how to improve your presentation skills with practice and planning.

What the assessors are looking for

It's important to be aware of what potential employers are looking for. Below are some of their priorities; you need to be able to:

- analyse and present key information effectively
- plan and manage your time
- organize and structure content
- show commercial awareness
- have an appealing delivery style
- demonstrate confidence

- engage with the audience
- use visual aids appropriately (if applicable)
- be able to handle questions or last minute changes smoothly

Everyone experiences some level of anxiety, however confident they may feel about presenting. The adrenaline rush of being in a competitive interview process is likely to have some impact on your delivery style. The better prepared you are the more you can relax and be present in the moment – showcasing your natural personality. Employers want to see what it would be like to work with you – they are not just interested in your impressive CV or long list of skills. They want to see your personality shine through and they will forgive some signs of nerves.

Preparation and delivery are both important. I can't emphasize this enough. How you say it is just as important as what you say – if not more so. Presentation is an art – the more you work on your style and approach the better you will get with experience.

Unplanned presentations

Sometimes you won't get advance notice of what you will be speaking about. The emphasis in this situation is often on testing how well you can think on your feet as opposed to delivering great content. Having to present without notice will most likely happen at some point in your career too.

You may be given a selection of topics to choose from on the day sometimes with as little as 15 minutes to prepare a five-minute presentation. This may sound intimidating, but there are many things you can still do to prepare in advance for this scenario.

One way is to find a friend or colleague to practise with. Get them to ask you impromptu questions so that you can practise preparing your talk at short notice and then deliver it in front of them. They can also give you feedback on your content and delivery. It doesn't matter what topics you use – the point is that you are simulating the interview presentation scenario by sticking to the time constraints and training your mind and body to get used to performing under pressure. I used this technique when I worked with the paralegal mentioned above.

The list of questions you get on the day could be totally random or linked to issues relevant to the company. Carry out some research by looking at the company website and news about trends within the industry to give you some background that may come in handy on the day.

The most important things to focus on are to use your short preparation time on the day to sketch out your key points with a strong opening line and conclusion. When you deliver the presentation, all your practise with the impromptu questions will help you engage with your audience. Much of the advice for planned presentations in the section below will apply to these unplanned situations as well.

Planned presentations

Usually you will have advance notice of what is expected in your presentation slot – this simulates typical real life work scenarios. Advance notice will give you the opportunity to prepare well.

Typically your slot will be 5–15 minutes long and you will be given a topic to prepare in advance. Whether you choose to use slides or not, the first step is to carry out research.

Research your audience and industry sector

When you receive details about timings and criteria for your assessment day or interview, go back and enquire about the assessment or interview panel. Try and find out who will be sitting in your audience as you deliver the presentation. This will help you plan your content and make it relevant to them.

It is helpful to assess the level of knowledge they have so that you can tailor your material accordingly.

If your topic relates to the company or your role then the obvious place to start is the company website as well as industry news as mentioned above. The presentation may be linked to the company's area of business – you may be given a problem or issue and be asked to come up with opinions or recommendations to report to a line manager.

The topics or scenarios you will be given will depend on the industry or sector you are applying to. The brief will typically highlight some kind of problem and ask you to recommend a course of action. For example, case studies may look like this:

- If you are applying for a Human Resources role, you might be asked to discuss what you might do if faced with poor performance.
- In a Business Development role you may be asked how and why you would improve the company business strategy for the next 3 years.
- In a Civil Service role a case scenario may be something like planning how to reach a target of reducing light pollution by encouraging people to turn off unnecessary lights at night.
- In manufacturing or engineering your case scenario may revolve around analysing a technical issue and recommending a course of action.
- In the legal sector, you may be discussing the impact of changes to an area of law

The purpose of a presentation in this context is to see how well you speak in front of groups so, although your knowledge of the subject matter is still very important, it is your structure and delivery that will be tested the most.

Once you have gathered background information, brainstorm your ideas on paper first, and create a mind map – don't leave anything out as it can come in useful later. Once you have all your ideas written out you are ready to put your structure together.

Alternatively you might have been asked to speak on a topic of your choice – if so, choose something you know about and are interested in. Avoid choosing something just because you think it will impress the panel. You might even be given a selection of topics to choose from, such as:

- introducing yourself and your background, covering how you have got to where you are now
- talking about a hobby or interest you are passionate about
- an achievement you are particularly proud of
- how you coped with a challenging situation

Pick a topic you can easily talk about. You're more likely to present more confidently if you feel comfortable with the content.

Structuring your content

Once you have gathered useful information about your given topic, you want to pinpoint your key points. Your time slot will be short: 5–15minutes. You can only focus on 2 or 3 key points in that time.

Design your material around the audience – what's in it for them? For example if your topic is 'tell us why you would be good for this role' rather than selling your skills, identify the business needs and show how your skills and experience meet those needs.

Next design a strong open and close. The opening grabs attention and the closing will be the last thing they hear from you. Both have to tie in with what matters to the audience.

Make sure you stick to simple clear language and terminology. They are not looking for how fantastic your vocabulary is. Some jargon may be appropriate – such as industry terms or ones specific to the organization. Using them demonstrates you have put extra effort into your preparation, but don't overdo it.

Once you have your core content and structure, think about bringing in stories or examples that will support your key points. They are much more engaging and memorable than just plain facts. More on this in Chapter 7.

Now that you have a clear skeleton structure, you can use it to build your slides if you choose to use any.

Slides and handouts

Check if you are required to prepare slides. Using PowerPoint slides simulates a typical business presentation setting but is not always necessary. A well delivered oral presentation that engages the audience is much better than a death by bullet point slide show any day. You may decide not to use slides at all but have handouts instead. Both slides and handouts are visual aids that will enhance understanding for your audience.

Slides are your support act. We look more closely at designing slides later in Chapter 9 but it is important to touch on this now. You only have a few minutes to present. The focus is on you – how you present, how confident you appear and how you engage the audience which may be a panel or just one assessor.

Rule of thumb – resist using too many slides and use very little text. Keep them clutter free. One of the biggest mistakes inexperienced presenters make is to crowd the slides with too much text. This is incredibly distracting for the audience and most of the time will bore them and they'll just switch off.

Anything you put onto a slide draws the audience's attention away from you. The same goes for slide transitions and animation. My personal view is to use very little animation and special effects for your slide transitions.

Many inexperienced presenters use their slides as a crutch to hide behind and also to help them remember what comes next. The slides are not a teleprompter or script for you. You want to aim for the opposite – bring the focus back to you and really connect with the audience.

Rehearse

Nothing will help improve your ability to deliver a great presentation more than practice. Rehearsal is essential. The trap that most people fall into is spending too much time creating slides and not enough time focusing on delivery. Even if you don't know what your topic will be in advance, you can still practise your delivery.

Timing is a very important factor. You want to nail it. If you have been given 10 mins then that is all you will have. Don't risk not finishing because you haven't prepared in the right way.

The best way to rehearse is to speak out loud and walk through your entire talk several times. Practice in front of others and get feedback. Mental rehearsal is not enough. If you are using slides – always rehearse with those.

Watch out for nervous energy and distracting body language. My views on body language are that, as long as your gestures are not distracting for your audience, do what feels natural. We look at these aspects in much more detail later. Rehearsing helps you deal with nervous energy as well as giving you a solid foundation so that you can better deal with any changes on the day or interruptions during your presentation.

Tune in to the audience and make appropriate eye contact. Aim to keep your tone and pace conversational. Natural delivery and humour come across as more confident and competent, but be careful how you introduce humour. Telling a joke is risky and few people can pull it off. You may want to instead use an amusing example or story to bring in humour without taking the risk.

Most of all, energy and enthusiasm are essential. You need to demonstrate you really want to be there.

Notes

Ideally you want to be so prepared that you don't need notes. But if you feel that you will relax more if you have some sort of notes, then make them work for you.

You want to aim for maximum audience connection. Anytime you look away to read your notes takes you away from your audience. If you decide you will be using notes on the day, then practise with them in advance. You want to maintain a conversational tone and make appropriate eye contact with the panel. Practise enough so that you are no longer reading from your notes word for word.

Some people find it reassuring to have their entire speech written out on A4 sheets so that they have everything they need close by in case they suffer a brain freeze. In reality that doesn't work because under pressure, it is almost impossible to pinpoint the exact point in your notes when you need it and it can actually hinder you. A much better way to use notes is to condense your material onto note cards, with only key words so that you can easily read them. Card is better than normal writing paper as there is less scope for highlighting shaky hands! Small envelope sized cards work well as they can sit in the palm of your hand discreetly.

Another way to use notes is to display your notes as a mind map on one single sheet of paper (like the one you might prepare in the research phase of your planning above) that can sit discreetly on a table near you or on the keyboard of your laptop. We'll look at mind maps more closely in Chapters 4 and 5 later.

Check logistics in advance

It's a good idea to find out what facilities will be available on the day as well as whom you will be presenting to.

Will there be a projector and laptop? Ask when you get there if you will be given time to set up eg during a break. It may not be possible to get into the room but at least by asking you are showing initiative and preparing as if it was a work presentation – you would want to check if everything will go smoothly wouldn't you?

Take a back up of your slides on a memory stick even if you are taking your own laptop to present from. One of the common pitfalls interviewees face is losing their slides or forgetting them. Make sure you clean up your desktop and shut down any mail or similar applications. Ask what kind of connection they have – it may be to a TV screen, projector or even wireless connection. If you are unable to connect your laptop at least you have your memory stick.

Have some form of timing device to help you keep to time. Either wear a watch or use the clock on your laptop or tablet as there may not be a clock in the room.

Take your mind map or an overview of your presentation with you in case your computer crashes. At least that way you will have a roadmap to work from.

Finally, you might want to consider taking a remote clicker with you. Whether you use your own laptop or one is provided for you, having the ability to move away from the keyboard will be incredibly beneficial. You won't know the layout of the room before you arrive and giving yourself the flexibility to move is helpful.

Questions

This part of the assessment is designed to test how you cope under pressure. Decide how you want to deal with questions. Tell your audience whether you are happy to take questions throughout or at the end.

The second biggest fear that people have after nerves about presenting is being caught out by a question they don't know the answer to. It is possible to plan for this in the same way as the main presentation. However, sometimes you just can't answer the question in that moment, either because you don't know or your mind has gone blank. That is perfectly normal – it happens to us all. The way to tackle this situation is to practise your version of 'I don't know' and say it with confidence.

Take the question section and turn it to your advantage. This is your opportunity to showcase your ability to think on your feet and bring in additional material that you just couldn't include in the presentation due to time constraints.

You can anticipate the types of questions you will be asked and be able to plan your response. The process you go through for researching and planning the presentation can be leveraged to help you with the question section. As you adapt your content to fit the audience, have a think about questions they may ask and prepare your answers in advance.

Your presentation slot

When you get into the presentation room – take your time to set up. Take a breath and pause. Only start when you feel ready. If you happen to slip up along the way then gather your thoughts and carry on – the way you recover counts for a lot. This is where all your rehearsal pays off.

TOP TIPS

- Plan your content and rehearse out loud – even if you haven't been given a topic in advance, make one up so you have some practice in rehearsing to the requirements set by the assessment centre and can develop some 'muscle memory'.

- Time your presentation – some recruiters will cut you off when your time is up so be prepared to finish within your time slot

- If you have planned your presentation in advance, take a tidied up version of your mind map with you.

- Keep a back-up of your slides on a memory stick.

- Take a remote clicker with you.

- Pin your note cards together in one corner so that if you drop them they remain in the correct order.

- Always ask for feedback afterwards – just like in the lawyer case study above.

3

GIVING PRESENTATIONS IN YOUR PROFESSIONAL LIFE: THE ESSENTIALS

Sharing information and communicating decisions through clear and persuasive presentations is a fundamental requirement for most jobs these days.

We live in a digital age where people's attention spans are very short – you are competing with people being tied to their devices and checking emails or social media even when they are in a meeting with you. That means you have to be able to cut through all the noise and capture their attention. The only way to do that is to master communication skills.

With every type of presentation, research and preparation are a must. How you deliver your message is just as important. In the rest of this book we take a deep dive into each of these aspects. Honing presentation skills is a lifelong commitment and it's never too early to begin.

The key to a successful presentation, whatever the context, is to clarify:

- Who the audience is
- What do they need to know in order to think or do something?
- Identify how best to tailor the presentation to the audience
- Have clear goals or outcomes – what do you want to achieve and what do you want the audience to do?
- Take the time to plan properly
- Always rehearse

Remember, when people give up their time to listen to you: make sure you value that.

Presentations in the workplace take on many forms ranging from sales presentations and pitches to training sessions and team meetings. Each one has a different purpose.

Information sharing and meetings

This is the most common every day scenario – giving updates or reporting on progress to your team, line manager or the Board of Directors. Day to day business revolves around teamwork, which means presenting to or on behalf of your team or department.

We spend a lot of time in meetings – whether they are face-to-face or conference calls. They can be a good way to keep everyone in the loop, but can also have a tendency to go off on a tangent and waste time. Conducted the right way, effective meetings can improve productivity and help move a business or project forward if they are planned well.

If you are in the early stages of your career, the chances are that you won't be setting the agenda but will most likely be asked to speak for a few minutes on a piece of work you are doing – to give a progress report or share knowledge with the rest of the team. While you can't control the entire meeting, you can take control of your bit – even if it is only five minutes. It is a speaking opportunity, one in which you can apply many of the tips in this book to such as structuring your content and even rehearsing what to say.

Networking and business development

In Chapter 1 we looked at how thinking of yourself as a brand and building a network can help support you in your career. Networking is also a key aspect of business development for many organizations. Business is about relationships. Networking events provide the opportunity to make connections or ask for introductions to decision makers in order to explore potential scope for working with each other.

Networking is a skill, one that not a lot of people are good at. Quite often you'll see people get stuck in one group all night because they don't really feel comfortable working the room and building rapport with strangers. They'll come away with a handful of business cards after an event and then not do anything with them. Being able to connect with people and follow up with them to develop ongoing relationships is part of the wider concept of effective communication.

Being able to explain what you or your organization can do or how you help your clients is not just for networking events. Part of the wider business development strategy includes client meetings over coffee or lunches or industry events such as conferences or seminars.

Managing and leading

As you gain seniority your levels of responsibility increase and you begin to manage others. Understanding how to get the best out of your team is incredibly important. Honing your presentation skills will help you chair team meetings, motivate team members and communicate more effectively with your colleagues and get results through working with people. Part of the role of a manager is to identify and deal with performance management issues and sometimes this means having tough conversations. Becoming an effective communicator helps you in those difficult situations. You will also get involved with a lot more meetings, many of which involve reporting to and getting buy in from senior managers. Again strong presentation skills are essential particularly as the stakes are higher too.

Presentation skills are important for leadership. If you think about famous leaders throughout history such as Winston Churchill or Martin Luther King, they all have the ability to inspire people to follow them using powerful presentation skills. I mention Steve Jobs (Apple CEO) as a case study throughout this book – he is very often referred to as one the best corporate speakers ever. Aside from the corporate speeches Steve gave in relation to product launches, he gave a very inspirational commencement address at Stanford University in 2005 sharing life lessons through three personal stories. Another example is Sheryl Sandberg (CFO of Facebook). Her TED talk and book *Lean In* has inspired a movement towards encouraging women to lean in to opportunities.

EXERCISE

Think about five leaders that you admire, either famous or within your own circle at work or in the community. What do you notice about their ability to speak to groups? How do they inspire and motivate?

Effective leaders are also effective speakers and influencers.

Delivering training

Some organizations have learning and development departments that organize staff training, but sometimes you have to take on the role of the trainer and deliver a workshop to your team or for clients.

At many of the law firms I worked with, sending someone on a course was a significant investment for the business. It wasn't just the cost of paying for the employee to go on the course but also the cost of the work they wouldn't be able to do that day. One of the ways in which this opportunity was maximized was to ask the employee to come back and share their knowledge from the course with team members either at the next team meeting or by hosting a mini workshop. This had many benefits such as encouraging knowledge sharing and presentation practice for the staff member who had been on the course. It is often said that teaching someone else new material is the best way to embed the learning for yourself. Another bonus is that you can become the go to person for a particular issue or topic, which in turn increases your reputation and visibility.

Pitching

If you tender for contracts and get to the final stages, very often the presentation stage is the deciding factor even if you are not the cheapest bid. Similarly, outside of the formal tender process potential customers want you to demonstrate why they should hire you over the competition when you both offer the same thing – what is it about your organization or team that is different? Being able to articulate this can mean the difference between winning a new client or losing the opportunity.

Speaking at conferences

This is a great opportunity to raise both your personal profile and that of your company. It is a chance to be seen in the market by competitors and potential clients. When you speak at events like these, you are perceived to have a certain level of expertise because not many people do it. However, not many people want to put themselves forward for this because they are anxious about getting up in front of peers and industry leaders and influencers. Yet that is the very thing that will help set you apart as an industry thought leader.

Public relations interviews

Giving interviews to press or media to give an expert opinion or share updates about a new product or service is a form of presentation. As with conference speaking, it helps raise your profile and that of the company.

Connecting with the wider community

In addition to delivering presentations to clients or prospective clients at external events, many organizations reach out to other sectors of the community. I sit on the Council of the Women's Engineering Society (WES) and part of the goal for the organization is to raise awareness of careers for women in STEM (science, technology, engineering and maths) related jobs. We actively encourage our

WES members to visit schools to give presentations to provide more information and inspire young adults to consider these types of careers. Young engineers regularly go out to schools and universities to give presentations to students.

Other examples include architects and local authorities presenting in partnership to residents in an area where a new development is proposed. This type of project has a big impact on people's lives and can be quite emotive. Presentations in this context have to be informative, sensitive and persuasive.

How mastering the art of presentations can boost your career

Throughout your career, you will come across many of these scenarios. The more senior you are the more you will be asked to speak and the more visible you are the better your opportunities are for promotion. When you are in the early stages of your career senior colleagues start to notice if you are able to communicate effectively through speaking in front of groups. Many people are good at their jobs, but not all are strong in presentation skills. Developing an all-round skillset can lead to being given more responsibility for client relationships and eventually getting involved in business development through pitching and conference speaking for example.

Building a reputation as a thought leader can lead to lucrative speaking opportunities. Conference organizers are always looking for great speakers. If we look at high profile examples in the business world, big names such as Richard Branson, Alan Sugar and Karren Brady all have reputations for being successful business leaders. They get paid a huge amount of money to give keynote speeches. If we look at sporting stars, big names get invited to speak at company events and conferences for a sizeable fee. But these are just the famous examples. There are many industry thought leaders that most of us don't know about because we are not involved in that area of work. Yet there are thousands of conferences that happen all over the world that need great speakers.

TOP TIPS

- Prepare for all your meetings by sketching out what you want to say and what you want your audience to come away with.
- Prepare for networking by rehearsing your introduction so that it is clear to the other person and invites them to ask more questions.
- Plan your path for career success and look for opportunities to speak in order to increase your reputation and visibility.
- Study leaders that you admire and analyse what they do to inspire and motivate their audience.

4

HOW TO PREPARE FOR A PRESENTATION

Our world is more fast-paced than ever. We are becoming used to having what we want instantly and it is having a significant impact on how we live and work. Against this backdrop it can be tempting to cut corners in your approach to presentations because time is so precious. However, the time you spend preparing, drafting, refining and rehearsing for your presentation will all pay valuable dividends.

When asked to present at work, many people think it's all about the slides. They see the slides as the focus of the presentation and so go immediately to PowerPoint (or any other slide software) and start typing in their content. This couldn't be further from the best place to start. Of course, slides can be important and can add value for your audience, but they are not always necessary. Try not to reach for the slides as a default and instead evaluate whether they will truly add value. If you do decide to use them, they should be created much further down the line so they can be designed to maximum effect. We'll learn about the steps to designing great slides in Chapter 9 but for now, as we focus on preparation, I want to encourage you to think about yourself and your message first. The slides are not the presentation – *you* are.

Why preparation matters

Giving a well prepared presentation is key to demonstrating that you care about both your message and your audience's experience. This helps you to be more persuasive and boosts your ability to win people over which, of course, has the important knock on effect of raising your profile and enhancing your career prospects. As you get more experienced, your preparation time will get shorter as you build up more efficiency and a bank of material you can repurpose (more on this skill later).

To impress future or current employers, you want to create content that persuades and makes an impact. But before we even start looking at content let's consider some sources and areas where you might find material to build your content around as part of the preparation process.

Research that will help you find material for your presentations

For your presentation to be truly useful, the right kind of research is essential. As someone who is ambitious and looking to take your career somewhere new, you may well already have your finger on the pulse of what's going on within an organization, an industry or what matters to particular stakeholders (stakeholders for you could be anyone from peers, managers, clients, suppliers or similar – basically anyone that is connected to what you do). However, it's important not to be over-confident: continuously improving your industry awareness through learning and researching will help you be a better presenter.

Here are some great sources for raw material to use as bases for a presentation:

- **Professional subscriptions:** If you have your heart set on entering a particular industry or if you're a current practitioner, having a subscription to an industry magazine or journal can give you deep insider knowledge of the latest trends, thought pieces and issues that will be relevant to your audience and can provide useful background context to your presentation (and some ammunition for difficult questions!)

- **Social Media:** Try and follow as many industry influencers as you can, particularly on Twitter and LinkedIn, in order to get great tips and links to important articles.

- **Key Word Searching:** Do a smart internet search with the key word and topics of your presentation to find the best websites, articles, reports in well regarded online publications, podcasts and videos. You don't need to include details from all of this research in your presentation itself: but having a deeper knowledge will benefit your overall knowledge and shine through when you are talking. There is so much free information accessible to you these days, you should never run out of inspiration.

- **TED Talks:** When preparing for your presentation, you can watch and learn from other speakers and get ideas on topics and different styles of delivery. I mention TED talks quite a bit in this book to help explain presentation techniques because they are freely accessible online and a powerful resource for studying presentation styles.

- **Films and Books:** These can be fantastic resources – they are not just there for entertainment! Sometimes a story or example from a film can help you add some spice to your presentation. We'll look at storytelling and putting complex information into context later on but, for now, this is a great way to get you thinking outside the box about how to source your material.

- **Speaking to People:** See if you can speak to an industry expert or someone with knowledge or insight into that particular area, whether at a networking event or over email. If you don't have access to anyone in your target industry, look closer to home. Consider your own network and whether any of your contacts in different industries could have some useful insight. There are always ways to find material to create great content for your presentation.

Keep a resource file

I want to encourage you to keep a resource file for your presentations. This is a valuable depository for ideas so that when you are asked to give a presentation or an opportunity to do so arises you aren't sitting there with a blank sheet of paper wondering where to start. This can particularly come in handy if a last-minute interview opportunity arises which requires a presentation or you have to do a presentation off-the-cuff in a professional scenario.

When you do find something you think would be great to use later, find a way to capture it. How often has a good idea popped into your mind and, though you've told yourself to make a mental note of it, you still find that the idea disappears as soon as you get involved in the next task? It might be a story, an interesting example a speaker shared in a presentation you attended, or an infographic you saw embedded in an article on social media during your commute. Whenever you get a light bulb moment like that, tag it or note it down somewhere.

I listen to a lot of different podcasts in my areas of interest ranging from Harvard Business Review to Social Media Marketing. If I hear anything that sounds like a good example I'll make a note to myself to bookmark it or record the idea somewhere. As soon as I can I'll type a text message or email to myself so that I can pick it up later and not forget. If I read articles online, I'll bookmark them or save them as PDFs so I can read them later. Same goes for newsletters that I sign up to. This practice has been incredibly useful to me in preparation of speeches and creating content for workshops. It helps me bring in interesting stories or facts that support my key messages.

My point is that whatever you stumble upon, if you like it, find a way to capture it for later reference. The low tech way to do it is keep a notebook and jot down ideas. There are also lots of digital sites that will let you curate your content such as:

- Evernote
- Pocket
- Feedly

By building a bank of useful material you can pull out items to fit almost any presentation scenario. Items of news, examples, research data and even stories can come in useful. We'll look at how to develop your own stories and add them to your resource file later when we get to Chapter 7.

Brainstorm ideas for your presentation

Once you have carried out your research, you are ready to sketch out some ideas for your topic. This is the stage where you write down all your ideas and thoughts about the topic – a brain dump.

At this stage think quantity over quality. If you edit too soon there is a danger your presentation will include more about what you want to share and less about what the audience needs to hear or will find useful. The best way to do this is to use a large blank sheet of paper – one without any lines. Turn it sideways (landscape rather than portrait) so that you have more space. Write your topic or key message in a bubble in the centre. Then as ideas develop draw branches off that central bubble until you end up with a spider diagram or mind map with lots of different sub topics or ideas grouped together.

This works well for those that are visual or creative. If you are used to working straight from your slide deck then this can be a little weird at first, but stick with it. After your first attempt, leave the sheet of paper to one side for a few days and come back to it. You'll be surprised at how much you can keep adding to it. Adding images to the branches enhances the process even more (though this of course may depend on the quality of your artistic skills!)

You may not have a few days to work on this phase because you have been asked to give a talk at very short notice or perhaps you are in an assessment scenario where you only have a few minutes to prepare rather than days or weeks. In these situations it is still worth sketching out your initial thoughts in this way – grouping similar ideas together. You can then home in and select your best points to build into your speech structure.

I personally use this process myself for all my presentations – whether they are 2 day workshops or 45 minute keynote speeches. After drawing several versions as my research expands, I condense it into a final clean copy with only key words or phrases mapped out in the order I will be speaking about (if you have good drawing skills, you could consider images too). This is my skeleton talk or blueprint that I can take with me to my talk. It is my back up if my slides fail to work and in case I suffer a brain freeze! I just leave it on the keyboard of the laptop that is playing the slide show or on a table nearby. I also carry it around with me in my bag so that I can look at it when I am travelling on the train or have a couple of minutes between meetings. That way I am reinforcing my memory with the content and running order so that I am much more ready to present without any notes at all when it matters.

I still keep the first version of my mind map – this has a lot more information on it than I can put into my presentation. This is useful background information that can help you prepare for answering questions or repurpose for another talk or even more detailed report.

Mind maps were made popular by author and TV presenter Tony Buzan. There are also plenty of other sources such as websites and books where you can find out more. If you have never seen a mind map before, have a look at some of the books on online stores to flick through some sample pages and see pictures of mind maps to give you a better idea.

One of the key benefits of using this method of planning is that you can group key themes or sub topics together branching off from a main idea.

Figure 4.1 shows an example I created using a free site called Mindmup.com:

In the above mind map I've taken the topic of 'how to succeed in your new job' and added sub topics as branches. This gives an overview of the key points. You can arrange them however you want and add different colours for levels of importance.

EXERCISE

Why don't you have a go at creating your own mind map? Pick a topic that is relevant to your role or organization or even an issue you feel strongly about outside of work.

There are now plenty of mind mapping tools and apps available if you want to do this electronically. The advantage of having a digital version is that you can edit it anytime without it getting too messy, have several versions and of course download for storage or printing.

Why rehearsal is essential for delivering a great presentation

There are many many reasons why rehearsing your presentation is a must and we will keep coming back to this topic throughout the book as it is such a fundamental part of successful presenting. Some key benefits are boosting confidence and keeping you to the allocated time slot. In this section, I want to

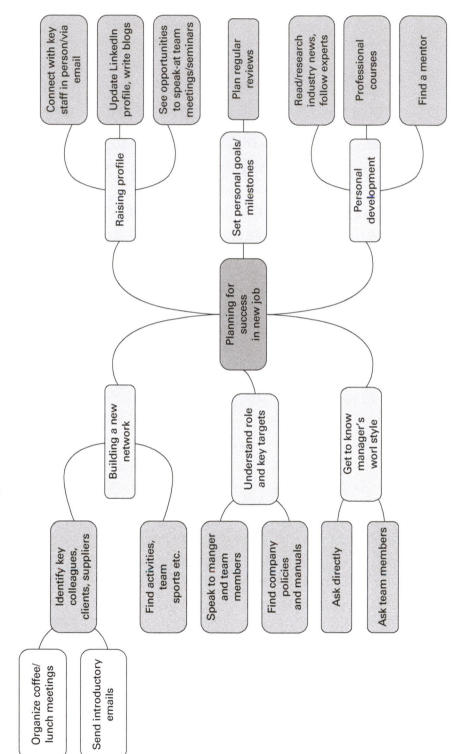

FIGURE 4.1 Example mind map created through Mindmup.com

convince you of the power of rehearsal to create a better audience experience. If you become familiar enough with your content and slide deck (should you choose to use slides), you'll be able to relax and concentrate on your delivery (rather than try to remember what part of your speech comes next). This is what gives you more confidence – the knowledge that you have prepared really well and can rely on that to keep you on track even when the nerves kick in. By going through several rehearsals, you can iron out any kinks but also it means that when you deliver your presentation for real it won't be for the first time – an unknown quantity. This goes a long way towards reducing nerves and gives you an opportunity to get a feel for what it's like to 'walk' through your presentation – how it feels to stand up at the front of the room, what your voice sounds like etc.

Can you wing it? I know plenty of people that try – some successfully – to give a presentation with zero preparation. Experience gives you the ability to wing a presentation to a certain extent, especially if you've become good at sketching out an outline at short notice and can rely on pre-prepared stories or examples that you have already tested out in front of an audience.

However, the vast majority of the times when inexperienced speakers try to wing presentations, it's obvious and the audience feels cheated by the lack of preparation. Remember why you are there – to persuade others and get buy in from them. In order to provide value to your audience you want to put in an appropriate amount of effort.

The more you practise the more muscle memory you develop. Think of it like going to the gym. After a few weeks or months you start to see the benefits and feel fitter and stronger. If you expect to get a six pack after one visit to the gym, it's never going to happen. Developing and honing your presentation skills is no different.

What if you don't have as much time as you would like because there are other pressing deadlines at work or you have been given very little time to prepare? Even if you 'walk' through your entire presentation at least once by speaking it out loud, it will be better than not rehearsing at all. In fact not many people put in the effort to rehearse to that extent, so whatever time you devote to this part of your preparation will set you streets apart from the average presenter.

If you are going to use slides then make sure you practise with those. This will help you become really familiar with the sequence of your slideshow which means you won't need to look back at the screen so much and can maintain eye contact with your audience.

Feedback

The only way you can find out what the audience sees and hears is to get feedback. One of the best ways to do this is to practise in front of colleagues or friends. They don't necessarily have to understand the industry area you are speaking about and actually if they know nothing about what you do and can still follow your presentation then you've probably pitched it right.

The important thing to remember about feedback is that it is just someone else's perception of what they experienced. What you choose to do with the information is entirely up to you. There is a lot of value in asking for feedback because we don't see the world in exactly the same way as someone else. Feedback gives you the opportunity to adjust and improve to better serve your audience – whether that is an Assessor or a Board of Directors.

Video and audio feedback is the next best thing – this is how you can see and hear what your audience does; it can be really enlightening. A good sense check is to watch the video with someone else to see if they think your performance reflects your natural personality and if your message comes across clearly. If you can bring yourself to video your rehearsal and watch it back you will see how you come across and how you sound – it is usually different to how we imagine ourselves projecting outwards. You may feel that your tone of voice is friendly and approachable but when you play it back it sounds too formal. Or, you keep fidgeting but had no idea until you watch it back. This type of feedback helps you make adjustments once they are brought to your conscious awareness.

It may make you cringe, but you don't ever have to show anyone else! When I was preparing for my TEDx talk a few years ago, I recorded my speech on my smartphone. I would then listen to it on my journeys into work with my headphones in. No one else could tell and I wasn't always listening consciously but the material was going in. This process helped me embed my content into my mind so I could work on my delivery on the day without having to remember what to say next.

Repurpose a previous presentation

Often, people will reuse a presentation previously delivered by a colleague. There is not necessarily anything wrong with this as there is no point in reinventing the wheel. However, make sure you check for any changes that need updating – such as processes, the law, statistics etc as well as checking whether there is any client sensitive information for example if you use the same slides for another client presentation. As mentioned above, the slides are not the presentation, you are so you can still personalize your content and delivery.

Longer term strategy for continuous improvement

If you want to get better over time, find regular opportunities to speak in front of an audience. Having these experiences is the best way to hone your skills for the long term.

Wherever you are currently working, look for opportunities to speak. Can you volunteer to give a short training presentation at a team meeting or put yourself forward for a client seminar your organization is hosting? Even if you can get yourself on the agenda at the next team meeting for a few minutes to cover an update of some sort it will give you more scope to keep working on your skills.

You could also join a speaking club like Toastmasters. If you haven't come across this organization before, Toastmasters International is a non-profit organization with speaking clubs in every major city of the world. For a small membership fee, you can become a club member and go along to weekly meetings to practise your speeches in front of a friendly and supportive audience. That does two things: you get used to speaking in front of groups and also get useful feedback that will help you to improve.

At the beginning of this book I shared my personal experience of having an irrational fear of speaking or presenting in public. One of the things that helped me on my journey of increasing confidence and improving my delivery was joining such a club. I was a member for a number of years and used that opportunity to work on my skills. As I became more experienced I started testing out parts of my professional speeches at the club to get some initial feedback – sort of like a stand up comedian does when they are testing new material.

The other benefit of a club like this as that at every meeting there is a section devoted to impromptu questions. Speakers are invited to speak for one minute on a topic that they are only given as they walk up to the front of the room. This is a brilliant way to get used to thinking on your feet. It helps you to prepare for coping with the questions you might get after delivering a workplace presentation.

Using notes in your presentation

There is nothing wrong with using them – just don't read from them. If you are going to use them make sure you practise with them so you get a feel for what it's like to have them in your hand and can get used to finding a balance between glancing down and then looking back up again to maintain eye contact.

For some people having the entire presentation typed up on A4 sheets is their version of a safety net. Here's the major problem with that – the text is too small and tightly packed together for the notes to be any use in that one crucial moment you need to find your place when you can't remember what comes next. Not only that, but if nerves are an issue then shaky hands become a lot more visible with paper sheets! This scenario is more common than you might think, even with senior executives. It is quite awkward for us in the audience to watch while the speaker gets anxious trying to find their place in the long text.

A much better way to utilize notes is to write key words on notecards – the size that easily sits within the palm of your hand. Use a big fat marker pen to write with so that your words are clearly visible when you look down briefly. Rather than writing full sentences, just jot down one or two words that will remind you what comes next. That way you can't get drawn into reading your text but have enough of a prompt there to keep you on track, should you need it. Chances are, if you have put in the time to prepare your content and gone through several dry runs, you won't need the notes anyway. They will just be there to reassure you. Top tip – clip your cards together in order so that even if you drop them, they will be in the order you need. I've seen people drop their notes a lot during the actual presentation and it is such an easy fix.

Another way to use notes is to have your mind map or skeleton cheat sheet described above.

It is also possible to use notes within your slideshow if you are presenting with slides. As you create your slides, you'll notice that under the slide you are working on there is a blank white section in which you can type anything you want. Some speakers use this area to put notes in. The advantage of incorporating notes in this way is that when you run through your slideshow in the presentation, only you can see them on your laptop as your 'presenter view' is different to that on the main projector or screen. The disadvantages are similar to those with paper notes – the text can be too small to read and you end up looking down, which breaks connection with the audience. In addition, you are tied to the laptop and can't move around. Depending on the setup of the room, the laptop may be fixed to a lectern or placed on a table in the corner of the room away from where you will be standing to speak. I personally don't recommend this way of using notes as it's quite risky, but everyone is different.

Go with whatever way you feel works best for you. The main thing is to prac-tise as much as you can with your notes so that your reliance on them is minimal and you get a feel for what it will be like to work with them.

Unseen presentations

Much of what I have shared above applies to unseen presentations just as much it does to those where you have advance notice and plenty of time to plan. What is different of course is that you won't know what topic you may get and will have much less time to prepare. You can still set yourself up for success by working on some of the suggestions in this chapter.

You can start building up your resource file so that you can pull out interest-ing material to talk about at short notice. While you may not be able to take your notes or any other kinds of resource file into the assessment centre it can still help to be better prepared. Typical topics that are set for presentation or problem solving tasks include:

- presenting a solution to a business problem
- creating a marketing plan from scratch
- discussing a new development in a particular industry

While you won't know exactly which topic or discussion points you will be given on the day, working to prepare for scenarios such as the ones set out above will give you some advantage. Think back to preparing for exams at school or university – you never really knew what you were going to get on the day so you prepared by becoming familiar with the course content and doing past papers.

Preparing for an unseen presentation is very similar. You can research the company website and get a lot of useful information from that, including their main commercial priorities and who their clients might be. You can also research what's going on in the industry or market space currently. Become familiar with that background information so that you can easily slot it into the task you are set on the day.

EXERCISE

If you are preparing for an assessment centre or interview – try to find out as much as you can about the role you are applying for and the organization – what potential problems they face, what they do well, who their target market is. From there, brainstorm some possible questions along the lines of the suggestions set out above and then get a friend to test you on them at random. You can simulate the strict timelines as well and create a mock presentation scenario where you only have 15 minutes to speak.

You can use the brainstorming technique to sketch out ideas, incorporating the information you have already become familiar with in your research beforehand – even if you only have a few minutes to prepare for example at the Assessment Centre. In the next chapter we look at how to structure your presentation and create a blueprint – you can use that technique in any situation and for both planned and unseen presentations.

Most importantly, you can begin working on your stage presence and delivery now by finding opportunities to speak and seeking feedback.

TOP TIPS

- Research your industry and topic – use social media, websites, blogs, newspapers, articles, podcasts, videos such as TED talks or on YouTube, as well as asking others for material.

- Use curating sites like Feedly or similar to collect or bookmark articles or blogs you can use later.

- Use mind maps or spider diagrams to brainstorm your content – resist the urge to edit at this stage.

- Always make time for rehearsal and feedback.

- Join a speaking club to get in regular practice.

- Seek out opportunities at work or outside to speak or contribute in meetings.

5

HOW TO STRUCTURE YOUR PRESENTATION

Once you have identified your audience's needs and the main messages you want to share, through your research and brainstorming, you can move on to structuring you content. You will inevitably have more information than you will be able to share so you have to choose the points you will focus on and structure them in a way that makes sense for the audience and builds towards your end point – the whole purpose of the presentation.

Structure is important for clarity and purpose. Without it you can end up rambling, risk losing the audience and lose the impact you were hoping to make.

Start with the end

This might not seem like the most logical place to start planning your presentation but think about what your intention for the audience is.

Do you want them to:

- take action or do something – for example adopt a new technique or way of working
- think differently or be inspired – such as supporting a csr (corporate social responsibility) project at work or get behind an innovative project
- behave differently – such as be willing share knowledge more openly across departments to better serve clients rather than worrying about losing a client relationship

Getting clear about this will help you plan out the rest of your presentation. There has to be a point to your presentation – an outcome. Something other than just sharing information. If you don't know your final destination, then it is very difficult to plot your way there – you risk rambling or worse failing to get your point across.

Opening and closing phrases

Your opening and closing phrases are your book ends and possibly the most important parts of the presentation. The opening should grab the audience's attention and the closing will be the last thing they hear so you want it to stick and make an impact. We'll look at these sections in more detail when we get to Chapter 10. For now keep in mind what you want to leave the audience with.

Once you have identified the objective or key takeaway for your audience, it's time to start putting your content together.

Choosing your key points or messages

In Chapter 4, we went through the brainstorming phase. Now you want to start trimming and pick only the content that supports your main points or key messages. This is the time to be ruthless.

Keep your content clutter free – think simple, clear points. There is no room for padding. Simple versus simplistic. By simple, I don't mean that you should dumb down your content. Just stay away from long wordy sentences and, unless strictly necessary, complex terms. Great presentations are easy to follow.

Imagine your audience are at point A before you share your presentation with them and you want to take them to point B when you finish. You want to include just enough content to take them to your end point B. Bridge that gap. No more and no less.

One of the most common mistakes presenters make is to include far too much content in their presentation. This is mostly because we feel compelled to share everything we know about that topic. Somehow, we think that it helps showcase how knowledgeable we are or that it adds credibility. We think this will impress people. It doesn't. What is does do is to overwhelm them. If you make your audience work too hard in having to sift through your content in order to get to the nuggets then you will lose them.

Typically, what assessors and interviewers are generally looking for in a candidate is the ability to distill key messages and put them across in a clear and persuasive way. Learning how to craft your content in this way will help you succeed. As you get along further in your career, being an effective communicator is a key skill to have as a manager and leader.

Resisting the temptation to cram in everything you know about a topic is one thing. Choosing which points to focus on and highlight within your presentation is another.

It also actually takes more time to hone your message for a shorter presentation than a longer one so make time to allow for this. As mentioned, one of the key problems that most people struggle with in workplace presentations is putting in too much information because they want to share all that knowledge with the audience. However, as discussed above, you only want to include as much as is necessary and no more to get your audience from A to B so that you don't overwhelm them. When your time slot for speaking is short, you need to be even more ruthless in trimming content and this can be challenging because you might believe the audience needs to know all the background but you can't physically fit it into the time you are given. Put yourself in their shoes and think about what they will find helpful rather than what you want to include. It could take a few drafts to get your content down to essentials.

In every given moment, we are bombarded with millions of bits of data – everything from the temperature of the air around us to trying to read text on your screen against a backdrop of multiple conversations in an open plan office. Your conscious mind can't cope with processing every minute detail and only chooses key data to focus on in order to deal with what is important in that moment. Why is this relevant to you in the context of presentations? Every single member of your audience will filter information in their own unique way and choose to focus on different things. When you craft your presentation you want to make sure you highlight the key messages and signpost them really well so that there is no ambiguity.

There is a fascinating video called the 'Monkey Business Illusion' that has been in circulation on YouTube since 2010 and is definitely worth watching. It's quite insightful and highlights how we all focus on different things even when exposed to the same circumstances.

Two teams are passing a basketball between them. One team are wearing white shirts and the other are wearing black shirts. The viewer is asked to count how many times the players in the white shirt pass the ball. While we are doing that a number of things are going on in the background. I won't spoil it for you in case you haven't come across this video before. Every time I have shown this video to groups most people miss something – and they all notice different things even though they have watched the same video! I have yet to come across anyone that has managed to spot all the changes first time.

The important lesson to take away from an experiment like this is that we need to guide our audience and help them focus on the key messages by keeping things simple and strengthening those points by signposting them effectively.

I can give you a simple example from my days as a young litigation lawyer. During that time, I dealt with a lot of road traffic accident cases and in order to investigate them I had to interview witnesses and obtain statements from them. Each witness would always give a slightly different account from the others. They all experienced the same event but remembered it slightly differently – whether that was the speed of the cars, the sequence of events or even the colour of the cars. It's not that they were giving inaccurate accounts in their minds: it was just how they saw the event and made sense of it.

This is important because we don't see the world as it is – we see it as we are, with our own personal filters and biases. We focus on aspects that we choose to pay attention to.

You might think you are being really clear but your audience may not have the level of knowledge you have or may not be as familiar with it as you. You will be very familiar with your content having gone through the preparation phase, but the audience might not – they may be hearing it for the first time. It helps to put yourself in their shoes when crafting your content. What knowledge do they have, will it make sense to them and is it easy to follow along from beginning to end?

For that reason, pick your best three to five points to include in your presentation. Less is more.

In the previous chapter we talked about rehearsing in front of others. This process is also valuable for testing out your material to find out if you have skipped over anything or included too much of something.

Why, what, how

Once you have identified the key points, you want to put them into some sort of order and then begin to add some colour to it by way of stories, images and data that support your message and bring it to life. But even before you get to that stage, think about why the audience should sit there and listen to you. What is their motivation?

In my experience, many business or workplace presentations focus on giving information without giving much thought to why it is important for the audience or how it will make a difference to them.

Why – this is quite possibly the most important section of your main content. Start your presentation here. This is the motivation part for your audience. They will be sitting there thinking 'what's in it for me?' (WIIFM) – why should they care? Remember that presentations are an investment of time for all parties. The presenter has a lot at stake and has invested time in preparing. The audience is giving up their valuable time to listen to you. The entire time they are in your audience they are not being productive.

This may be where you highlight your 'why'. In an interview or pitch situation you want to persuade them to hire you or your company. So this is multilevel because even when you are mindful of you personal 'why' you still need to tie it in with their WIIFM. For example if they hire you what will they gain as a company? At an interview, the question or topic you are given might not be as obvious as 'why should we hire you?' It could be something like how you might solve a problem or your opinion on an industry trend or changes in the industry. Focus the 'why' around the importance for the panel or organization.

What – this is the section most of us find the easiest to approach and where we tend to focus. The nuts and bolts of your topic. The content that includes fact and logic. This is of course important, but until you hook your audience in with why this information is important to them, you might struggle to get their attention. I have sat through many presentations, and I'm sure you have too, where the speaker has just gone through endless slides giving facts or information without tying it back into the purpose of the presentation – the call to action or end destination. This part does not need to be long. Remember you are taking your audience from A to B. Include only enough content to enable them to join up the dots. If you have got a lot of useful background information then hold it back and share it later or in some other way such as a more detailed report or handout after the talk.

How – here you describe how what you have shared will affect them. What can they do with the information you have given or how can they put it into practice. How will your message affect them/help them or make a difference?

For example, let's look at this in the context of a typical task at an assessment centre, which could be framed like this:

Overview

A national company is about to introduce a new pricing structure across its entire client base. This will be implemented through a new software platform – up until now the process had been manual. For years, customer pricing was ad hoc, sometimes at the discretion of regional managers. This impacted profit and efficiency. Some customers are also not happy as there is disparity between their respective contracts. All staff need to be familiar with this change and have to come along to a presentation where more details will be given.

Exercise

Deliver a presentation discussing how the new pricing structure will be adopted

The presentation could be set out like this:

Why

The team needs to know about this new structure and system so they will be better informed to talk to existing customers and deal with any concerns (some customers are going to end up paying more now, while others will benefit by paying less). This new system will make it much easier to talk to potential new customers as there is no room for confusion. The software will make billing much simpler – so less work in the long run.

What

A breakdown of the new pricing model – easily explained in a chart. Possibly also comparing the old pricing structure with the new to highlight the benefit.

How

An initial demonstration of the new pricing software platform will give everyone a feel for it and then they can go away and test it in their own time to become comfortable with it before the launch date.

At an assessment centre you might be asked to consider a business scenario and then come up with a strategy or make recommendations. Once you have identified your recommendations (remember start with the end) you can tailor that to why it's important to the panel, what the strategy is and how you suggest it is implemented.

Most presentation topics lend themselves to this sort of structure, even non work related topics. However, if for some reason, you struggle to break your topic down into these sections, at least focus on beginning with the 'why' WIIFM for the audience. You can craft your opening around the why section with techniques for grabbing their attention. More on this in Chapter 10.

After sorting your content into these three sections, you can begin to build upon the raw material by adding colour in the form of stories and examples. One way to go about this is to create a story board. This concept comes from the movie industry – a graphical representation of how a scene will unfold, frame by frame.

I use sticky notes to create my version of a story board. I'll write one key point on each sticky note then arrange them in the right order. Next I'll go to my resource file and look for stories or examples I've collected or created earlier and write the relevant ones onto sticky notes. Once I have all the moving parts of a presentation I can play around with the order until it feels absolutely right. This works much better than having to rewrite a script every time I want to make changes. The sticky notes can go on a wall, desk or even a sheet of paper – easy to move them around while scoping out my talk. Storyboarding gives you a high level overview and helps you order your thoughts.

If you prefer, creating a mind map as shown in Chapter 4 or flow-chart for your presentation is an effective alternative to storyboarding. (See Figure 5.1.) Whatever works for you. Basically we are creating a roadmap for your entire presentation. Creating this type of framework lets you wing it within that structure. Let me explain. This structure is the same whether I am speaking for ten minutes or 90 minutes. The longer version just has more stories and examples in it.

FIGURE 5.1 Flow chart alternative to mind map 4.1

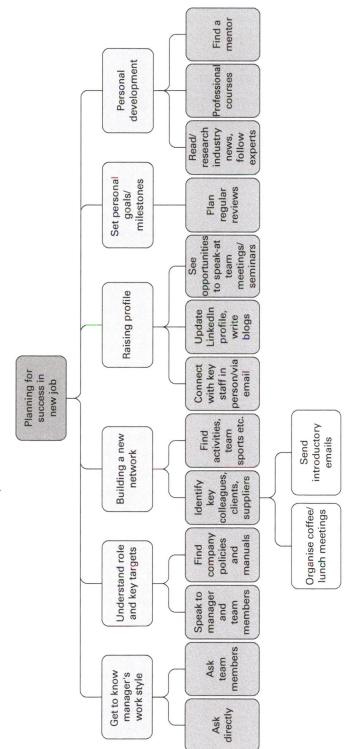

TOP TIPS

- Start with the end then reverse engineer your content.

- Block out time to prepare your presentation.

- Choose your best 3 points to focus upon.

- Keep it simple and easy to follow.

- Use the *Why, What, How* format to organize your content.

6

TIME MANAGEMENT

While this chapter is titled 'Time management', in reality we can't manage time – everyone has the same 24 hours in a day to play with. What's important is how we utilize the time we each have – we can only manage our priorities. In the context of delivering presentations, we need to consider personal priorities and those of others such as your audience and event organizers.

Why timing your presentations is essential

In workplace presentations, the timing of your talk is very important. Whether you are speaking at a meeting or giving a formal presentation, you will be given a time slot. Few people have any idea how much they can cover in the time they have been given to deliver a presentation. This is something that comes with experience and, of course, rehearsal.

Here are some issues that typically arise when people go on for too long:

- In a multi-speaker conference the day is carefully planned. If a speaker goes on for too long, they can get interrupted and asked to stop at a point that is not a natural end for their talk. This can lead to a premature or rushed ending. Neither is ideal. Another negative effect is that if you go over time, it will have an impact on the rest of the schedule meaning that someone else may have to cut their speech short. A badly timed presentation can appear disrespectful to the organizers and the other speakers. Your timings can have further reaching consequences too: a 20 minute delay on a pre-lunch presentation can cause chaos for catering staff and a grumpy audience.
- At team meetings where there is a planned agenda, each item or speaker is give a time slot. If anyone goes over time, someone else has to adjust or the meeting has to run longer to get through everything on the agenda. This gives a bad impression because people have other priorities, whether it is

arrangements with important clients or other meetings. Not only that, but if your presentation goes on for too long, people will start to look at their watches, lose patience and stop listening.

- At an assessment centre or interview everyone is given a time slot. Unlike in a team meeting where there may be scope for the meeting to run over, here the speaker will be asked to stop or wrap it up when they get to the end of their slot. You could potentially waste your opportunity to win the panel over by not preparing well. You also don't want to test their patience by going on too long – it can work against you by leaving a negative impression. The other factor to bear in mind here is that tasks set at assessment centres are strictly timed – for example 15 minutes for a presentation. By keeping to within your designated time slot not only are you being respectful of your audience and getting your point across, you're also demonstrating that you have the ability to manage time. This is an essential skill set that recruiters look for in candidates.

It seems obvious to say that if you go over time, it's not a good situation to be in. You risk annoying others and rushing through your content which means you don't create the impact you intended. I hope I have persuaded you to not want to be *that* kind of speaker!

People's time is valuable – respect that. Anytime they are in a room with you, they are not elsewhere completing their normal work. You'll lose the audience if you go on too long.

We talked quite a bit about the benefits of rehearsal in the previous chapter. Here the focus is on getting your talk down to an optimum time – one that fits your designated time slot. Unless you time your rehearsal while speaking out loud, how can you ever know how long your speech will last? When you rehearse, always time yourself.

Sometimes you will be given even less time than you have prepared for, possibly because a colleague or another speaker has gone over time or another item is added to the agenda. If you have prepared and planned your talk in sections, then you will know how long each one is. If asked at short notice to speak for less time than planned, you need to know how much to cut. You can do this in your head when you are prepared enough. For example you can cut one of your stories or case studies because you know that it would take 5 minutes to share it and you need to trim your talk by that much.

If you go online and look at TED talks, you'll notice they are all 18 minutes or less. This is so that people focus on getting their message across in a short amount of time. The organizers found that 18 minutes worked well because it's roughly the amount of time you might spend on a coffee break – most of us can easily find time to watch an entire talk if it's that short. All TED speakers have to stick to the strict time slot and prepare accordingly – it doesn't matter if they are celebrities or politicians, the rule is the same for all the speakers.

Toastmasters is a great example of speaking to time. Each prepared speech delivered at the club has to be between 5 – 7 minutes. There is a traffic light timing system at the back of the room usually with a set of different coloured lights or sheets of card that are held up for the speaker to see. The green light goes on at 5 minutes, the amber light goes on at 6 minutes and the red light goes on at 7 minutes. If the speaker goes beyond this they are interrupted and asked to stop. This is a great way to learn how to speak to time.

Toastmasters also hold an international speech contest every year. In 2016, 30,000 people entered the competition worldwide at their respective clubs and through regional and national rounds this number was whittled down until ultimately there was one winner – the world champion of public speaking. The 2016 champion is a young lawyer from Singapore called Darren Tay. He comes on stage and pauses for a significant amount of time – causing the audience to sit up and take notice. Then he pulls on a pair of white underpants *over* his suit and immediately gets a huge laugh from the audience – it is unexpected. This is his visual aid, his prop. There are no slides – just him and the underpants. The speech is centred on the topic of bullying and how Darren coped with that. Even though the issue is serious he weaves in humorous anecdotes to create that contrast of light and shade. Every single part of this speech is timed and rehearsed down to within a few seconds – from the length of the dramatic pause in the beginning to each individual story. What is of particular interest is the fact that when he looks at his watch and draws attention to the five minute mark in his speech it is exactly five minutes. He is *that* prepared. He has to be. The strict guidelines for this contest state that even if you are one second beyond the seven minute thirty second cut-off there is an automatic disqualification. The stakes are high here – most winners hope go on to launch a career as a professional speaker. The finalists have invested too many months of preparation and rehearsal to risk going over time.

Have a look at his speech on YouTube – you'll notice that the total length is just less than seven minutes and thirty seconds.

Of course we aren't all able to devote that level of preparation for a workplace presentation but how important are the stakes for you? I would encourage you to put in as much preparation as you can in order to deliver an engaging presentation within the allocated time slot.

Choosing how long to speak for

I've focused a lot in this chapter about how important it is to stick to time in order to manage the expectations of your audience and event organizers. This is where the time slot has been set for you. What about situations where you get to decide how long you want to speak for? You might be asked to give a short presentation at a team meeting about a course you attended recently – sharing that knowledge with the team. Or, you may be invited to visit a client and give an update on new processes or improved products. How will you determine the length of your presentation?

We audiences are difficult to keep engaged for long periods of time if the content and delivery are not interesting to us. The amount of time is not so much as important as the way in which you utilize it. Longer talks need more variety by way of stories, videos or audience interaction for example. You want to avoid monotony as it encourages people's mind to wander.

In later chapters we look at techniques such as storytelling and interaction to help you better engage your audience. When it comes to identifying the length of your talk, the first place to start it by structuring your message. Remember that your job is to take your audience from A to B and include only as much information as they need to think or do something differently – whatever your objective for the presentation is. This will help you decide how long your presentation needs to be.

Keeping on track during your presentation

Obviously if you have prepared enough you know exactly how long you will be speaking for. It's still a good idea to know how you are doing against the clock in case you are asked to adjust your speech last minute or there are unexpected interruptions etc. It would be ideal if there is a wall clock in your line of sight – just check that it is set at the right time.

You might wear a watch – this is a little trickier to work with as looking at your watch can signal you want to get your speech over with. If you can take it off and keep on a table nearby within sight that would work better. Alternatively you can use apps for your phone or tablet that will count down. Again you can place this somewhere nearby. The other option is to ask someone in the back of the room to give you a five minute or two minute warning by holding up a notecard. Just remember to look in their direction!

Managing your time in relation to preparation

It might have become fairly obvious to you by now that preparing a presentation takes quite a bit of time. I have suggested ways to make the process more efficient going forward by creating a skeleton framework and building a bank of pre-prepared stories. But the process is still time intensive. In your busy schedule how can you make space for all this? Often it will involve prep time out of office hours. Everyone works in their own way. For me, I break my prep time down into chunks – sometimes half an hour twice a week if I have a long lead-in time to a presentation. Short bursts of concentration work well for me. For you it might be different. What is important is to schedule designated prep time into your diary otherwise it doesn't happen and you end up having to wing it.

Having a few slots spread over time is hugely beneficial as it lets your unconscious mind keep on processing. You start to get even more ideas as you go through several drafts and the end product ends up even better.

Managing your time at the assessment centre

Depending on the set up for the day, you may well be involved in a number of activities such as group work as well as presenting. If you have been given your topic ahead of time, then you will be ready to deliver your presentation when you arrive with no extra time needed to prepare.

However if you're only given your topic on the day, you will have some time to prepare. Whatever preparation time you do have, use it wisely. Allocate time for each section of your preparation from reading the brief, to highlighting key messages, preparing a skeleton outline with your why/what/how and also rehearing. Even if you only have 20 minutes in total to prepare, leave 5 minutes at the end to go off somewhere quiet to walk through your talk and say it out loud at least once.

With any of these scenarios, it all comes down to the same thing. The more you control timings the more control you have over finishing strong and not having to miss out or rush the end of your presentation.

TOP TIPS
- Diarize time to plan your preparation.
- Break down your preparation into manageable segments.
- Practice enough to know how long your presentation will last.
- Know how long each segment of your talk is so that you can quickly think on your feet and cut if necessary at short notice.
- Find a device you can rely on to check on timings during your talk.
- Ask someone to give to give you the heads up as you near the end of your slot so you can wrap up with impact.

7

PRESENTATION STYLES AND TECHNIQUES

The image that comes to mind when workplace presentations are mentioned is that of a PowerPoint slide presentation that is mostly full of text and quite often hard to follow as the material can seem quite dry. However this does not have to be the case at all. There are many ways in which any presentation can be brought to life by introducing techniques such as storytelling and well-chosen examples that make your content 'sticky' and better engage your audience.

Different types of presentations

Different styles can be used to connect with audiences in different ways, from motivational formal keynote speeches that inspire to training workshops that teach the audience new concepts or techniques.

Keynote speeches are less detailed and more entertainment focused. They will typically be 45 minutes to 90 minutes long and are inspirational or motivational in nature, with a lot of emphasis on storytelling. You will see keynote speeches at conferences or awards dinners for example, where there are large audiences. The speaker usually doesn't have any slides – it is more of a performance with just them speaking with very little interaction with the audience. The style required for a keynote speech will vary depending on the kind of event – if it's an after dinner speech then it will be entertaining and for a daytime conference for national sales representatives for example, it may need to be more motivational. You might not quite be at this level yet with your speaking but, if you continue to master your presentation skills and excel in your professional life, giving a keynote speech could be an achievable ambition.

Internal company presentations or sales pitches for example, cover more detail, are information based and geared towards smaller audiences so have more opportunities for interaction. This type of presentation could be an update to the team or department or a pitch to a new client. Use of slides here tends to be the norm. The style required for an internal company presentation will vary according its purpose and topic. Sometimes a more fact and data based style works better and sometimes a more emotional and creative style is more appropriate or a blend of both. In order to determine how to adapt your style you need to analyse what the audience expects – this comes back to researching and tailoring your material to your audience, more on this in Chapter 18.

Workshops will be more instructional with lots of information but also a lot more audience interaction as well, through activities and discussion.

These are just some of the ways in which you may encounter presentations in the workplace – from formal to informal. In addition to the various formats, there are also various techniques that can be incorporated into any of the scenarios above:

- Using visuals such as slides and props can really enhance a presentation if used the right way. We'll go over this aspect in Chapter 9.
- Incorporating storytelling and analogies to illustrate points by giving examples or anecdotes connecting to learning points are very powerful and provide an opportunity to show emotions.
- Humour is a great way to engage your audience. If you can make your audience laugh it goes a long way towards keeping them engaged. This is not a technique that works for everyone though so, as I've said in previous chapters, be aware of the risks.
- Putting complex information such as financial data into context by using everyday examples makes it more accessible for the audience.

Then there is individual style. There's not necessarily a right way to deliver a presentation or a preferred style but some of the ideas in this chapter will help you in finding ways to engage your audience and develop your own style through experimenting with the recommended techniques and adjusting as you get feedback from your audience – as discussed in Chapter 4.

The power of storytelling

According to an urban myth, American novelist Ernest Hemingway one day made a bet with his fellow writers that he could write a story in six words. He collected ten dollars from each of this friends and wrote his six-word story on a napkin:

For sale: Baby shoes, never worn.

The validity of whether this scenario actually happened has been challenged by many and it's even been alleged that in actual fact this particular short story appeared as a newspaper advert in the classifieds section. Whether there is any truth in the Hemingway anecdote or not, the short story itself is an interesting example to consider further.

When you read the short sentence what do you think has happened? What is the full extent of the story? The reason behind putting the shoes up for sale could be any of the following:

- They are an unwanted gift.
- They were bought for a girl but the baby was a boy.
- They were the wrong size.
- The baby had too many shoes.

Those are just some ways in which to interpret the background of this story and there could be many more. That is the beauty of storytelling – you let the audience go into their own worlds to fill in the gaps.

Throughout history, human beings have been learning through storytelling. It is one of the best ways to share knowledge and information and at the same time, making it memorable. I was once in a lecture where the Professor told us that people came up to him all the time to tell him they remembered a story he had told them perhaps months or even years ago. The professor laughed as he said that it was remarkable that people remembered his stories so vividly – he couldn't remember where he was or when he'd told them!

Try and recall five presentations or speeches you have been to. Can you remember the main points? Most people struggle to do this because generally our memory fades over time. Quite possibly the presentation itself was not that effective in highlighting the key points. If you do remember anything, was it because it was wrapped in a story? Like the professor example above, we are more likely to remember stories than information.

How you can use stories in your own way

You may be thinking that you don't have any stories that are interesting or relate to workplace scenarios. I want to challenge you to think differently.

A great example to look at is Sir Ken Robinson, who has one of the most-viewed talks on TED – *Do Schools Kill Creativity?* I'll keep coming back to this particular talk as it is a brilliant example of how to incorporate storytelling into a business presentation.

Within the first five minutes Ken shares two very short stories – one is a personal story about his four-year-old son in a nativity play and the other is a story someone told him recently about a little girl drawing a picture. Neither of the stories are particularly remarkable in themselves. That's the point – they are everyday examples. The common theme is about little children not being afraid of making mistakes. What Ken does with these short stories is to weave them around the serious point he makes. He uses the stories as hooks.

You can develop your own stories and use them in the same way as Ken does. Think about everyday examples at work or life outside of work that you might be able to tie in with a key message or lesson – jot down some ideas that you could develop into stories.

When creating your stories you will go through a few stages. First write out a draft in full and resist the urge to edit at this stage. You just want to get all your points down for now. Then leave it for a few days before you come back to it and start to edit.

I like to think of this process of crafting your story as if you are writing a joke. A comedian will write and refine a joke over many weeks or months to get it right – the idea is to set up the joke and get to the punchline or pay-off as quickly and as efficiently as possible. That's what you want to aim for in your story – get to the pay-off as fast as possible. Think about what your end point will be. It's just like structuring the content for your entire presentation that we looked at in Chapter 5 – getting your audience from point A to point B by only including what is absolutely necessary. Nothing more and nothing less. Ideally you want your story to be between 1 and 3 minutes. If you watch Ken Robinson's TED talk you'll notice that both stories within the first 5 minutes of his talk are very short and take us straight into the scene. Like a good movie that opens in the middle of the action.

By going through this editing process over several sittings you will be able to refine the story so that there is no padding in it – just enough content the help the audience get involved in the scene. The other major benefit is that you become really familiar with the story – you memorize it.

How might you choose the type of story to include? It will depend upon what feelings you want to invoke in the audience. Do you want to make them laugh and be entertained as in a keynote or after dinner speech? You may want people to feel a little scared so that they take notice for example on the topic of cyber security or make them feel proud in an annual round-up of the team's achievements. Getting an emotional reaction can propel people to take action or feel motivated – you can do this with your stories. A short story can be incorporated to elevate even the driest of topics such as financial or legal updates.

Start building a bank of stories so that you have material you can use later. The idea is to learn once and use many times.

If you haven't used stories in your presentations before, start small with just one and then commit to adding it to your next presentation.

EXERCISE

Have a go at writing a story. I'll give you a topic to get you started:

What is the biggest challenge you've ever had to overcome?

This is the type of question you often come across in interview situations. If you take some time to develop your answer as a short story here, you will have some material to call up if you are ever put on the spot with this question in future.

Depending on where you are in your career you will have various sources of experience to draw from. It could be work related, a sports achievement or a personal challenge.

Client case studies are also a great source of material – they don't even have to be projects that you have personally been involved in. An obvious example is quite often in a sales pitch, teams will showcase successful client case studies – this adds creditability to the pitch and instils confidence in the prospective client.

You can also borrow stories – again look at Ken Robinson's TED example. One story was from his own personal experience and the other was a story he had recently heard. You can get inspiration from books, films, news, sports, history – literally anywhere. If the story is something you can tie in with your message and the audience can relate to it then use it – just don't pass it off as your own. I'll often use examples from film/TV shows or TED talks in my speeches if I think my audience are aware of them or they are topical. Many of the books I read on leadership have interesting case studies which I also refer to from time to time – obviously crediting the source where appropriate.

The power of analogies

Sometimes, ideas that are difficult to put across can be better explained using concepts the audience is already familiar with by way of metaphors or analogies. They are figures of speech in which reference is made to one thing in order to explain another – used as tools of comparison to help us understand things better. Analogies highlight the similarity between two things, metaphors compare an existing thing to another unrelated object or situation.

The main point here is to think about how you can use these types of comparisons to help describe things that make sense for your audience.

In a later chapter we'll look at designing slides. Slides feature quite heavily in business or workplace presentations and the most popular software used is PowerPoint. Over the years I've seen many people use PowerPoint in an ineffective way – usually by cramming in too much text in bullet points. In actual fact, it is possible to create amazing slides that can enhance your presentations if you know what to do. PowerPoint has many functions that most people just don't know about.

When I talk about this problem in my presentations I'll use an analogy: 'Imagine owning a Ferrari and only driving it at 20 miles per hour. Most people use PowerPoint the same way – they just don't understand the potential.' Using examples like this help make your content stickier and more memorable.

We are using these tools in our everyday language anyway without really thinking about it. Here are some familiar phrases using sporting terms:

- Keep changing the goal posts (implying the terms have been changed unfairly)
- Dropped the ball (referring to making a mistake)
- Jumping the gun (setting off too early)
- It's a marathon not a sprint (longterm benefit versus short-term gain)
- Ballpark figure (rough estimate)

These types of phrases or examples can help your audience reframe a problem or situation with a new perspective, making the strange more familiar.

Using humour to engage your audience

Adding humour to your talk will make it much more engaging. By humour, I don't mean telling jokes. Some people can pull off telling jokes in a presentation setting but it is a risky strategy. If you are good at telling jokes then that's fine, but there has to be a link between the joke and the point you are making. I've seen many speakers tell a joke just to break the ice at the beginning of the presentation but it's not the most effective way to grab audience attention. We'll look at openings in detail in Chapter 10.

A great way to bring in humour is through stories. You don't have to be a comedian or naturally funny. It's all in the delivery.

Let's go back to the Ken Robinson's TED talk. Both of the stories at the beginning get laughs. His delivery is very conversational and engaging. As he is sharing his story he pauses just before the funny line in the story. He has clearly spent a lot of time developing the content with just the right amount of emphasis in his delivery. This is something which comes with adequate preparation and experience.

Your entire speech doesn't have to be funny. Just bringing in a light hearted story or example to break up the speech can be very effective in drawing the audience in and creating some contrast to a serious subject matter.

You can also use slides to bring in humour. In her TED talk *Your Body Language Shapes Who You Are,* Amy Cuddy uses funny images and video footage of famous politicians to add humour and illustrate her point at the same time. Most of the talk is serious with a lot of technical data as well as a personal story at the end, but there are flashes of humour. This is another good TED talk to watch on the topic of how body language affects how we see ourselves and how others see us. It has been viewed over 40 million times.

For more examples on how to weave in humour for serious topics, check out some of the competition speeches for the annual Toastmasters speech contests on YouTube. Some of the most popular ones are Dananjaya Hettiarachchi, the 2014 winner, and Darren LaCroix, the 2001 winner. The format for these speeches are based around the hero's journey – overcoming obstacles and coming to a life changing realization which is not the typical business scenario. What is relevant though is the way in which these speakers use everyday amusing stories or examples and link them to the serious subject matter.

Putting data into context

Another key technique for improving audience experience is putting facts and figures into context. It is quite common to see figures and technical information in workplace presentations – from sales performance and financial growth to detailed specification for products. This type of information is used to support key messages or prove a point. The trouble is that too often we get blinded by science. What I mean by that is that many presenters think that using lots of graphs or bullet points listing statistics adds credibility. It actually just confuses the audience. Having said that, there are of course presentations that by definition have to include hard data such as reporting to the company board or updating a sales team. It is still important to think about context even where the bulk of the content is based around numbers and statistics.

The message here is to keep things simple and clear. Numbers on their own don't mean much with context.

A great speaker to look at is Steve Jobs, former CEO of Apple. He is considered to be one of the best corporate speakers in recent history. Every time Apple launched a new product he would deliver a great presentation showcasing the features and benefits.

For each product launch over the years, the presentation covered detailed technical data. Steve provided this for all those audience members that wanted it but he also did something else. He put data next to an everyday example that everyone in the audience could relate to.

When the iPod was first launched, he talked about how this new device could hold 1000 songs. Prior to this, MP3 players could not hold many songs. We get the idea – this new product can store more songs than anything else that we can buy in the market, but what does 1000 songs look like? He went to say it was like storing 1000 songs in your pocket on something the size of a deck of cards. I often use this example to help people understand the power of putting information into context and if I'm using slides, I create something like the example in Figure 7.1 to make it more visual for my audience.

Similarly, when the MacBook Air was announced as the world's thinnest notebook, it was pitched as so thin it could fit into an office envelope. On that occasion Steve Jobs stood on stage in front of the audience and literally pulled the MacBook Air out of a brown office envelope. He told us how thin it was and then he showed us by putting it next to (or in this case inside) something tangible – an everyday example we can all relate to. We in the audience can now visualize how much space that notebook will take up in our bags for example.

Many of Apple's product launches are on YouTube – take a look and see how Steve Jobs put data into context.

Think about how you can use context to make your material more memorable. By using this concept of putting complex information next to something more tangible, you not only make it more interesting for the audience it also helps the material stick in their minds.

Some time ago, I worked with a client who was a senior manager in the food and beverage sector. He was working on a presentation that focused on reducing product waste in all their retail outlets and cutting costs by doing so. One of the products was milk. Over a period of time many gallons of milk were being thrown away for various reasons. He could have just told the audience how many gallons of milk were wasted over a 12 month period. Instead he chose to introduce audience interaction by asking them to guess how many gallons of milk fill an Olympic size swimming pool and then he landed the punch by telling them that the waste over the last few months was the equivalent of an Olympic pool. The mental image is more impactful than just saying how many gallons – much easier to remember.

FIGURE 7.1

There are many different presentation formats and many techniques to enhance them. The way in which you use some or all of the techniques is up to you – based on the experience you want to create for your audience and your personal preferences. Take what works and leave what doesn't. The only way to really find out is to test it out.

TOP TIPS

- Start observing situations around you and look for ideas to develop into stories.
- Watch TED talks and Toastmaster Speeches for examples of storytelling and humour.
- Capture ideas to use later – whenever you see or read something interesting that may be useful material for you, make a note of it somewhere.
- Draft your story in full and then edit in stages over a period of time.
- Use analogies to compare something complex to something the audience is familiar with.
- Put your data next to an everyday object for the audience to relate to – keep it simple and don't overwhelm the audience with too much data.

8

PRESENTING AS PART OF A GROUP

Presenting as part of a group or team requires the same fundamental techniques as presenting solo. You need to set clear objectives, have a logical structure, prepare well and deliver the presentation in a way that engages the audience. However, presenting in a group does also come with unique challenges. There are a lot of moving parts to consider, egos to manage and a lot of important decisions to make together very quickly. With proper planning though, you can make a group presentation a great success. As we've seen, preparation is essential but, when it comes to team presentations, it is even more so.

Group exercises at the assessment centre

In the world of work, there are many instances in which teams are asked to present their work as a group. This is one of the reasons why group presentation tasks can appear as part of assessment centres. Group exercises are a common selection technique, especially when recruiting for positions that require collaboration and team work.

The group exercise may vary but is most often designed around a work related problem within the specific industry. The format might be a presentation, discussion, role play or problem solving exercise.

The focus of this chapter is on doing a presentation as a group, but all of the skills and techniques outlined here will also be relevant to other group activities where you have to show effective communication, including:

- problem solving tasks that test how the team coordinates and pulls through the best contribution from each team member.

- discussion tasks that involve looking at a workplace issue and agreeing steps to resolving the problem.

- role play tasks that could be a mock meeting in which each member is given a particular role to play within the meeting in order to meet objectives.

Ground rules for assessment centre group presentations

In this section, I'll cover some points that are specifically relevant to group presentations at an assessment centre. The rest of this chapter will cover more ground in relation to group presentations overall.

When you get to the assessment centre, if you are being tested in a group scenario, you'll most likely be put into a team with people you have never met before. Introduce yourself and, if the team is shy, invite the others to do the same in order to break the ice. Even though you may all be competing for the same role, it is important to think of yourself as a collaborator rather than a competitor.

It's about finding the fine balance of being vocal enough so that you are seen to be putting your point across and not stealing the limelight by talking over or ignoring others in the group. The assessors will be impressed by you facilitating team work. If there are any areas of disagreement, deal with them tactfully. For example, someone may say something you do not agree with. Resist giving critical feedback or dismissing the idea or comment shared.

The same principle applies of course in the workplace.

There are many aspects that are being tested when group tasks are set:

- active listening
- communicating – the ability to express ideas clearly
- collaboration and working as a team
- planning and project management
- leadership potential and ability to persuade and influence
- ability to deal with pressure
- decisiveness
- confidence

All of the above come into play when presenting as part of a group. For example listening to each other speaking is important to ensure content is consistent and there is little repetition – if you only have a short amount of time to prepare the group presentation each speaker is bound to go off track a little. By listening intently, you can think on your feet and adapt your own content. If you are properly tuned in to all the speakers in your group you will be better prepared for questions at the end from the assessors. The smooth transitions between speakers demonstrate good collaboration as does stepping in to help with information if one of your team members freezes as they are presenting their slot.

You might be asked by the panel how you worked together and who came up with the format and ideas of your group presentation to elicit who shows leadership and project management skills. You might also be observed as you are planning as a group and so it's helpful to bear this in mind and get into the team spirit.

Key points to cover for group presentations

The advantages of being part of a presentation team are shared responsibility, more expertise available to field questions and showcasing the capabilities of the team. There is strength in numbers. The challenge, however, is being able to integrate materials and presentation styles.

What you want to achieve is a smooth and coherent end product rather than individual presentations that are knitted together. This tends to happen when each speaker goes off on their own to work on their 'bit' in isolation. All the presenters need to collaborate in order to deliver one seamless presentation. Avoid a mix of styles and tone. Think of it in terms of an orchestra playing in harmony – individually each member is amazing but if they don't work together from the same sheet of music the sound can be out of sync and not a good experience for the audience. The best way to achieve this is to have at least one run through with everyone giving individual feedback to the rest of the group as to any adjustments that need to be made.

In a group presentation sometimes there is no appointed leader and you may want to make the first move. Someone has to be the project leader otherwise there is no one to ensure the following points are taken care of:

- coordinating the team
- using everyone's talent
- order of the content
- congruency in delivery and message without any overlap
- smooth transitions between all the speakers
- sharing air time – balancing achieving the task with your own agenda

Scenarios for group presentations

A group of individuals are often brought together for a project and will be asked to present the results when the project has finished or are put together to bid for new work in a competitive pitch situation.

Let me give you some examples of team presentation scenarios in practice.

The business consultancy

I often work with MBA candidates – most of whom have been working in their respective industries for a number of years. As part of their course they gain experience of business consultancy, working on real life client cases requiring project work and group presentations – with demanding blue chip clients. It is an opportunity for students to apply their academic knowledge and industry experience to an actual business situation.

Their challenge is to solve a real life business issue, utilising project management skills to deliver a solution on time and within budget. They then make recommendations that the clients can action. Projects range from carrying out feasibility studies for the company to enter into foreign markets to investigating the impact of new technology in healthcare.

Not only are these team presentations important from the client's perspective, but each candidate is marked by their tutors for the MBA qualification as well – twice the pressure which means they need to understand the value of preparation. In a way, some of the challenges that arise in the assessment centre are relevant for these students as well – in particular making sure everyone is seen to be contributing at the same time as presenting a clear solution for the clients. I always encourage the teams to work on their presentations together in one room to ensure the final project is not disjointed in any way. Finding the time to practise is extremely difficult due to the demands on the MBA, but this is the only way to ensure a smooth and professional-looking presentation.

The tender presentation

During my time at a law firm, there were regular tenders for new client contracts. Tendering is a long and intensive process involving many individuals within the organization, including a dedicated bids team, the lead partners who would be working with the client and several supporting staff members.

On one particular occasion, after successfully getting through the document submission stage, the team was shortlisted to deliver a presentation. There was a lot riding on this opportunity. Many hours had been spent gathering data and putting a persuasive pitch together in a lengthy and detailed document. Much of this work had to be done in addition to the, already demanding, 'day job'. Due to intense work commitments, getting everyone together to work on the project had been almost impossible, but proved to be completely necessary.

In the process of tendering, though price can be a major influencing factor in the client's decision, most often it is not the company with the cheapest bid that will be successful in winning the contract. The live presentation is an opportunity for the shortlisted companies to reinforce why they should be the ones to succeed, make a unique impression on the client and tackle any concerns the client may have. It's a chance to demonstrate what it would be like to work together.

The presentation stage can be make or break. It can be the difference between winning or losing a contract – which, of course, can have a significant knock-on effect on the organization as a whole.

The emphasis is very much on teamwork. Sometimes the team has to put in long hours to get every member up to speed and create a presentation that will persuade the prospective client.

As soon as the date for the presentation was confirmed, decisions had to be made about who would be part of the presentation team and what content would be covered. Then we divided up the content and distributed it to the speakers who were best suited to delivering that particular element. We also agreed on how we would tackle questions at the end. The pitch presentation is an opportunity for the clients to ask for clarification on anything that isn't quite clear from the tender document – or to put the team under pressure by asking how they would deal with particular challenges.

On the actual day of the presentation, our team were the last ones to present at the very end of the day. Walking in, we passed the previous team as they were leaving. Each of them had a confident smile on their face. You can imagine how nervous we were: so much was at stake but our competitor team looked like they'd knocked it out of the park! Not only that, when they walked into the presentation room, the judging panel looked tired – they had been there all day listening to pitches. These are the kind of pre-presentation blips that can affect your confidence.

Luckily our team had put in a lot of preparation and had planned for the lack of energy in the room as well as the tough questions that followed. We managed to turn a difficult situation around. Our bid was not the cheapest but our presentation helped us win the contract. What got us through was that every single individual was on the same page and had recognized the value of rehearsing in front of each other and receiving collaborative feedback. That level of effort and attention to detail paid off.

The website design pitch

Another organization I worked with is in the business of designing beautiful user interfaces for client websites. When they take on a new client, they spend a lot of time getting to know the company to better understand what they want to achieve, their culture and their expected outcomes. Most of their clients do not understand the ins and out of web design. What they want is a user friendly website that looks great.

When the team have a meeting with a prospective client, they will typically take someone from business development, someone from marketing and at least one of the web design team with technical expertise. They all need to be up to speed with the project so that they can sell their services in a way that will appeal to the prospective client – each person will speak about their area of responsibility in the project in turn and then be available for specific questions. Just like in the examples above, the team spends a lot of time preparing and rehearsing their sales pitch.

You may not ever get involved with situations like this but could be involved in internal projects for example rolling out new training, explaining changes in policies or procedures, installing new equipment or software, marketing or social media campaigns. Remember that team presentations require more effort and more time to plan.

Planning your group presentation

In any team presentation, someone should take the lead and be the project manager to take care of the following:

- Clarify objectives
- Identify team strengths and delegate accordingly
- Manage timings
- Make decisions about content and order
- Allocate a timekeeper
- Decide how to deal with questions
- Decide how to deal with introductions

In the context of an assessment centre group activity, the first task of course is to choose a team leader – this is necessary as otherwise you end up having a free for all approach and risk not covering key task objectives. Whoever takes on this role, not only needs to take care of covering the aspects listed above, but also has to be able to deal with common group problems such as dominant person-alities and disputes over the topic or how to structure the presentation. This is a group task so everyone will have an equal stake and must pull their weight, how-ever there needs to be someone that makes final decisions once the group has expressed their individual opinions. Should you put yourself forward? Don't fall into the trap of thinking that you need to be the leader for the assessors to notice you – they are observing you all anyway and you can demonstrate leadership skills through collaborating, listening and coming up with good suggestions.

One way of approaching selection of the group leader is to ask everyone to give a brief explanation as to why they would be good for the role – like in The Apprentice TV show! Then you can take a vote. If you don't want to lead in that particular task because you don't feel confident enough then tactfully say that you think another member of the group is better qualified because they have perhaps more project management experience or relevant knowledge of the topic but that you would whole heartedly support them. If you do end up leading then think about setting some ground rules. Explain how you will deal with any disagreements – will you make a decision or ask the group to vote? Remind everyone that you are working against the clock and it's in everyone's best interests to cooperate.

Much of this is also applicable to workplace group presentations. As mentioned above, you want to think of the project as one cohesive presentation rather than everyone going off and creating content for their own section and turning up on the day of the presentation without having rehearsed together.

Aim to create an overall plan – then divide it up into sections according to areas of experience or skill. Divide your content into logical sections – sometimes this means some sections will be longer than others. Obviously this will be trickier at the assessment centre as it's important to get a fair balance of stage time for all group members. It may not be possible to get agreement on every single aspect – compromise and then focus.

In addition to creating a master script, create a master slide deck with the same fonts, colours, headings and language. That way even if everyone designs their own section of slides they will have the same look and feel running throughout.

Introducing each speaker

Moving from one speaker to the next can be awkward if not planned well. There are several ways you can address this. Each speaker can summarize their piece briefly and then hand over to the next speaker, by saying something like:

'Now that I've explained about the aim of the project and what we hope to achieve, Amy will explain what needs to happen in stage one'

The next person then picks up the narrative where the other speaker left off.

Or you can have someone go through a brief team introduction right at the beginning – either one person does this or each team member introduces themselves.

There is no right or wrong way – the key point here is to be decisive about how you will tackle introductions as a team and then rehearse doing that. Just keep the introductions brief.

Seamless transitions between speakers

Think about the physical space – where will everyone sit or stand? When it is your turn to speak how will you get to the front in the least disruptive way? Remember to factor in the time you need to walk to the front – will there be an awkward silence while people get into position? If so, think what you could do to minimize that.

Decide who will move the slides on – will you pass the remote clicker onto the next speaker as you finish your segment or is it better to have one person in charge of moving all the slides on for everyone?

Pay attention to each other even when you are not speaking. Just because you aren't speaking at one moment doesn't mean you aren't being watched. Pay attention to the current speaker and make sure you look engaged and interested. There is nothing worse than seeing other team members checking their phones when their bit is over. The other benefit of staying alert is that should anyone have a problem with slides or remembering content, one of you can step in and rescue them.

Rehearsal and practice

In the examples I gave above, I've already discussed the importance of rehearsing as a team as often as possible. This will help you come up with a back up plan and getting familiar with every part of the presentation means that you can step in if someone drops out or loses their place. Almost like having an understudy in a play! You want to aim for a similar level of energy from one speaker to the next in the final version. Also, make sure you practise on your own as well so you don't let the team down.

Questions and answers section

If you are presenting as a group, the likelihood is that there will be questions from your audience. Come up with a list of possible questions and divide them up so that each team member can prepare. Decide how you will field questions – best if one person does this by allocating questions to appropriate team members rather than everyone jumping on a question together or worse no one saying anything because they think someone else will. Practice keeping your answers short and to the point.

Getting better at group presentations

It is always better to put in the ground work and get some practice in before you do get called upon to be part of a group presentation. Practice with friends or colleagues by making up a realistic group topic.

This may not always be possible so you might want to use past experience to help you get more insights.

Think back to opportunities you had to present in groups at college or university. Walk through those in your mind and conduct a debrief. Use that past experience as a case study and analyse that in the light of the recommendations made in this chapter – what would you do differently if you had to give that presentation again now? In Chapter 4 we looked at the value of feedback and carrying out a debrief every time you deliver a presentation. The same technique applies here – you are just going back further in time!

TOP TIPS

- Break the ice with group members at the assessment centre – think about collaboration as opposed to competition.
- Discuss the content as a group and divide it according to team strengths.
- Create a master slide deck that is consistent through each segment.
- Decide on how to create smooth transitions including team introductions.
- Agree on how to tackle questions.
- Rehearse together and give each other feedback.

9

USING TECHNOLOGY AND VISUAL AIDS

The use of visual aids, particularly in the form of slides, is commonplace in workplace or business presentations – they cover everything from low-tech paper handouts to embedded videos within a slide deck. I want to stress that the emphasis should always be on the content and delivery in any presentation however, adding in an extra medium through slides or props can improve the audience experience. The framework should come first and adding in multimedia should come second.

How to decide what to use

When most people think of a professional presentation, PowerPoint slides immediately spring to mind. However, it is important to deeply consider what you are talking about before even thinking of the visual component.

Visual aids can be your support act and give your audience:

- Something to look at, which is very important for people that like to receive information visually

- A way in which to make better sense of complex information such as data

- Variety – in order to keep them engaged, it helps to mix up your delivery

Using well-chosen visuals can be a very powerful way to enhance your message and make it more memorable. We tend to retain information better when it's shared both visually and orally.

'A picture can paint a thousand words'

You'll have probably heard this phrase before. What it means is that our minds can process images much faster than written words. Not only that, when you use an image to support a key message or story, it allows the audience to make sense of it in their own imagination. The image acts as hook.

Slides could be your visual element, but not necessarily. They are your support act. People don't come to see your slideshow, they come to hear you. Yet this is one of the biggest mistakes many presenters make – they believe that a presentation is the slide deck and begin their preparation by typing straight into PowerPoint, without much time or effort devoted to audience experience and delivery. They also think that the slides are there to keep them on track and help them remember what comes next when they are speaking – using the slides as a sort of teleprompter. That is not what slides are for.

There are of course other ways in which you can introduce visual content. You can use props, hand-outs or a flip chart. To decide what to use, think about the number of people in your audience. While delivering a prepared slideshow in an interview situation to only two or three people might feel natural for that scenario, doing this in front of the same number of people in a meeting scenario might feel like overkill. However, if slides truly enhance what you're saying then they can still work in any context: you might just choose to be seated while delivering them sometimes.

In smaller settings some of the low tech options like flip charts or hand-outs may be a better option as they are more interactive (but could also come across as unprofessional if you work in a highly corporate environment). As with anything, it's always best to use your common sense. What works is usually common sense.

Remember this – *you* are the presentation; not your slides or any other material you choose to use.

Slide design for maximum impact

People often make the assumption that using slides makes the presentation look more professional. That is not necessarily true. In fact, improper use of slides can make your presentation look bad.

It is challenging for audiences to do two things at the same time – read your slides as well as listen to you. By putting a slide up on the screen, you are drawing their attention to that and each time you bring up a new slide, the same thing happens. Whatever you put up onto a slide for your audience to look at or read, be aware that they will need time to process it. The aim therefore is to keep the slides very simple and design something that can be processed by your audience in seconds.

In addition to creating slides for your own presentations, quite often you'll be asked by senior managers to create slides for their presentations as they are usually too busy to do this themselves. It will be your job to understand what their vision is and try to interpret that by creating something that reflects the message they want to convey. Or, your team may outsource this step and engage external designers to the create slides if there is a budget for that and the occasion is important enough for example a conference speech or investor pitch. Whatever the scenario, if you are involved in helping to put together slides for someone else, the tips in this chapter will support you in that.

Before you even open up PowerPoint, take a look at your storyboard or skeleton outline of your speech. Use that to scope out how many slides you need to support each point and what you might want to put into each slide. Start with outlining a framework for your slide deck. What are the key points you want to highlight? Can they benefit from a visual image to reinforce your point? At this stage just sketch out an outline of the number of slides you want and roughly what you are going to put on each. When you have that, you can think about what pictures or graphics you want to use. You don't need a slide for every single part of your speech.

Approach your slide creation with a design mind set. Treat every single slide as a blank canvas and only add content to it that will look good, is absolutely necessary for the audience to understand your point and actually enhances their experience.

We'll focus on PowerPoint in this chapter as that is still the most commonly used presentation software in the business world. If you work for a creative or entrepreneurial organization then you might use Keynote for Mac or Prezi perhaps. Whatever your preferred presentation tool, the tips and suggestions here apply to all.

If you take away just one tip from this chapter it's this:

Avoid filling your slides with slabs of text!

It is quite a common urge for speakers to want to include everything they know about a topic onto the slides – to showcase their knowledge and also because they think that is where the value is: providing lots of content. If you do that, you risk losing your audience, subjecting them to 'death by PowerPoint'. The slides are not documents but they often get used in that way. A better way to share useful information in detail is by providing a hand out. More on this later. For now, think less is more when it comes to slides. Every bit of real estate on each slide has to have a purpose. Anything else should be stripped away.

I often advise start-up companies on getting ready to present to potential investors. The investors often like to see the slides in advance of the presentation meeting. Ordinarily, if you have done your job right, then the slides will have very little text and not mean much without you the presenter being there to put them in context. However, in order for the investors to be able to make sense of the slides before the live meeting, some text has to go onto the slides. When the company arrive for the presentation, that text is removed – effectively they create two different versions of the deck: a read deck and a presentation deck. Since we are focusing on presentation skills, your slides shouldn't be a *read* deck but a more visual and minimalist *presentation* deck.

Not only do want to be ruthless about what you put onto each slide, you need to be mindful of how the slide will look when projected onto a big screen or TV. The test is 'can the person in the back row see this clearly?' What looks fine on your laptop screen will not necessarily look good on the large screen. Keep to one idea per slide. If you need to use more slides to develop a point do that instead of crowding too much information onto one slide.

I often get asked, how many slides is optimum? That is a difficult question to answer as it depends. Most of the time, I would say a common sense approach is best – if you are using 100 slides for a 20-minute presentation then that is probably too much. It's not so much the number of slides but the way in which you use them. If each slide is very minimalist and you can click through them really quickly and discretely while still connecting with your audience then you might be able to get away with more slides. I've seen some of the most effective and persuasive presenters use just one impactful slide to set the tone and then talk around that slide.

Take a look at Nancy Duarte's TED talk for examples on creating simple slides with very little text and purposeful use of images to set the scene. Nancy is a presentation expert and author of *Slide:ology*. Also, look up Slideshare for more examples of how others create slides.

If you are using text, keep it very short so that it is possible to skim read it and still follow you as you speak. A better way to use content is to swap your text for well-chosen images or graphics to help your audience process the points you are making much quicker.

Here are some specific tips to help you get the most out of PowerPoint.

How to blank your screen during the presentation

You don't ever want to leave slides up on a screen longer than necessary. Once that particular slide has served its purpose, either move on to the next one or blank your screen. If you leave something up there that is not directly relevant to what you are talking about in that particular moment, it serves as a distraction for the audience. If you press W on your keyboard it turns your screen white. To bring the slides back up again just press the same key again. If you prefer a black screen, just hit the B key and it works in exactly the same way. This is a much more effective way to keep bringing the audience back to you. What you do need to remember to do is bring the blanked-out slides back up when you move on to your next point! This is something you absolutely need to rehearse doing as in the heat of the moment during a presentation, it can be easy to forget you have blanked your screen if you are not used to doing it.

Colour and contrast

This is not something that people think about but has a huge impact on the audience experience. What looks good on your screen as you design your slides on your laptop doesn't always translate well to the big picture projected in the presentation room. You won't always know what the lighting will be like in the room you will be presenting in even if it's the usual meeting room in which your weekly team meetings happen. Natural light coming in from windows can make the screen less visible. It helps to test out your slideshow in the meeting room in advance to see how they will look and whether the lighting will have any effect.

But what about if you can't get into the room to test your slides for example if you are presenting at an interview or assessment centre? The best way to control this is to use the right type of contrast between the slide background and the colour of font you use. In normal office lighting, a light coloured slide background such as white with dark text on it works fine. If the room is bright you might want to use a dark coloured slide background and light coloured text. Even if you can't get into the actual room you'll be speaking in, test your slides by projecting them somewhere similar. If you have gone to all the trouble of creating meaningful slides then you want to make sure your audience can see them as you intended.

Slide transitions and animations

Slide transition is the special effects applied as you move from one slide to another. There are lots of options in the menu bar within PowerPoint under the 'transitions' tab – anything from flying in to exploding in flames. They can be fun but also very distracting. Depending on your audience, using these types of transitions can come across as not very professional. My personal preference is not to use any slide transitions – I think simply clicking from one slide to the next is just fine. If you do use transitions, keep to the same style throughout the entire presentation to be consistent.

Similarly you can use animation effects for individual parts of your slide. For example when explaining a sequence, you may want to bring in one line of text at a time to lead the audience through the content step by step. Again, in the menu bar you can select a range of different types of animation effects as you bring in new parts to a slide. I would suggest keeping things consistent and using only one or two styles of animation as otherwise you end up with a haphazard looking slideshow.

Your choice for the above options should be guided by the culture of your organization and the audience you are speaking to. If delivering a prepared presentation at an interview, consider the options that will best showcase your unique skills and impress the interviewers. If delivering to colleagues or superiors, consider what their personal preferences might be and use that to inform your choice.

Font style and size

Think about the style of font you choose for the titles and text in your slides. Again this is a matter of personal choice but you may be influenced by house style or branding guidelines. Your company may be conservative or laid back and you want to pick something that reflects the culture and image. Whatever you choose, pick something that pops out from the screen and is easy to read. The test is whether the person in the back of the room can see it. Fonts that are recognized as being professional, clear and simple are Arial, Calibri, Helvetica, Century Gothic, and Verdana.

For simple and effective slides, limit your choice to a maximum of two different styles – you want a smooth consistent look across the entire deck.

The size of font needs to be big enough so that it can be read easily on the big screen. What looks clear to you on your laptop doesn't necessarily look that great when projected. I would suggest a minimum size of 28 point.

Using good-quality images

It's not too difficult to create visually appealing slides. Wherever possible, replace text with a photo or graphic. With less text on your slide you are free to talk about your key points without being restrained by a script.

How can you decide what sort of images to use? Go back to your slide outline and find something that will create a link to the key message for each slide. Photos work really well, especially when you are sharing a story. Choose a concept image to support a story – you can use it to set the scene and leave it up on the screen as you tell the story. Make sure you always use high-quality images that are not pixelated or distorted. When you insert them into your slide, always use 'full bleed' – ie fill the entire slide with the photo without any titles or logos.

If you want to add a key phrase or simple quote, rather than type it into the heading insert a text box over the full image – it creates a much more polished effect. You can find the option to insert text boxes under the 'insert' dropdown on your main menu at the top of your PowerPoint screen. Once you select the text box, PowerPoint positions the cursor onto your slide – just start typing your phrase without clicking away, otherwise it can look as if your text box has disappeared. Once you have something typed in, you can edit the font style and size as well as drag the box to sit over any part of your photo.

Using shapes, flowcharts and graphs to display data

Earlier we looked at putting numbers into context for example putting big numbers next to everyday examples to help your audience visualize what that figure really means. The same concept applies to designing your slides.

Replacing bullet points with a visual graphic is much easier for the audience to follow and also more memorable. Using shapes such as pie charts, simple bar charts or flow diagrams can help illustrate complex concepts – they help put data such as statistics or percentages into context. Avoid using small text on the axes if you are using graphs – think about how it will look for the person in the back of the room.

See the example of how to convert a bullet point slide into a simple flowchart below. I've used a basic example of how to explain the sequence of events for a delivery driver as most of us these days can relate to ordering items online and organizing delivery.

You can create these types of graphics within your PowerPoint slide by selecting 'shapes' from your menu bar. Another great resource is Canva.com – there is a free version and a paid version. Your imagination is your only limit to creating simple yet effective graphics that can bring your material alive. This particular flow chart uses standard shapes for processes, as the topic relates to a process; however, you can use any shape you like to create flow charts in your presentation if it helps make your content more visual and easy to follow.

Grouping images and shapes

This is a really useful function that not many people are not aware of. It is one of the best ways to make sure that any moving parts on your slide remain where they should be. For example if you have created a graphic with lots of shapes sitting next to each other in sequence or in layers, then the risk is that they can get messed up if you try to play your slide show on another computer. If you take your slides saved on a memory stick to an external venue such as an assessment centre, it is highly possible that they have a different version of PowerPoint than the one you used at home. This can cause your text boxes and other shapes to become misaligned which is not good. What you want to do is lock all the parts of your slide or diagram into one master image. To do this, click 'edit' and 'select all' capturing all the parts, then find 'group' under the 'arrange' button on your toolbar. This may be in a slightly different place on your version of PowerPoint such as under 'format' or 'drawing tools' but it will be there somewhere.

For an in depth look at advanced techniques I recommend taking a look at the support section from the creators of the software, but the tips in this chapter should be enough to help you craft a polished and professional presentation.

Resources for images and copyright

Sourcing photographs can be challenging if you don't know where to look. Many people search for pictures on the internet and the copy and paste them into their slides. The problem with that is that someone owns that image and you

FIGURE 9.1 Delivery driver process

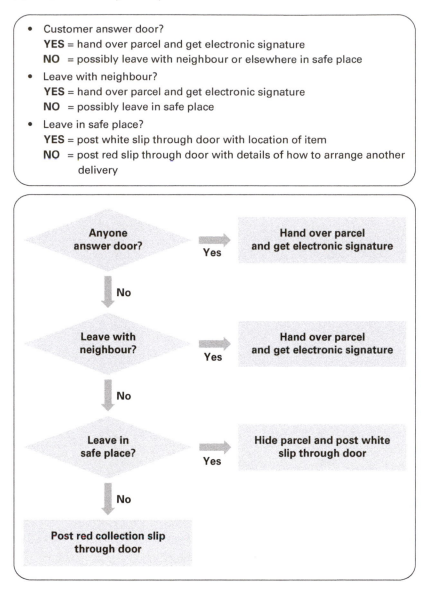

- Customer answer door?
  YES = hand over parcel and get electronic signature
  NO = possibly leave with neighbour or elsewhere in safe place
- Leave with neighbour?
  YES = hand over parcel and get electronic signature
  NO = possibly leave in safe place
- Leave in safe place?
  YES = post white slip through door with location of item
  NO = post red slip through door with details of how to arrange another delivery

can't use it without getting permission – they are subject to copyright law. I would discourage you from grabbing pictures in this way and instead get them from sites where you can download 'royalty free' images (where you have the appropriate permission to use the images). Some of these sites offer images at no cost and others charge you a one-off fee or offer you an annual licence. At the end of this chapter I'll list a selection of these sites where you can get royalty free pictures.

The best option is to take your own photos (though exercise discretion if they feature people in them) – that way you don't need permission.

EXERCISE

Have a go at creating some visual slides by inserting images with text boxes over them similar to the example above. Play around with the styles of font and colour to see what works best. Take a look at some of the image resource sites listed below and download a few of them. You might also want to create a free account with Canva.com and explore their graphics library before creating your own images that you can then download for free. They also have 'how to' tutorials to give you guidance.

Videos

Another way to make your content more visual is to use video clips that you can embed into a slide. They can be useful in helping you create an emotional connection with your audience. Again check for copyright permissions if you are using someone else's video.

As with photos, you can create your own video content. This can be getting sound bites from clients or experts. Using customer testimonials in a sales pitch is quite a common way to introduce social proof and credibility into a presentation.

Another way to use video is to create an animated infographic within PowerPoint. Take a look at the support sections for in depth guidelines or tutorials to find out how to create these.

Flip charts and whiteboards

When you have a small group, using a slideshow may be too formal. Flip charts or whiteboards, are low tech and need very little advance preparation plus they create a more interactive dynamic.

If you are delivering a presentation then you can write out you main points or if your drawing skills are good, sketch out images or flow charts as you go. You can also draw out images in pencil in advance and then go over them in pen in real time during your presentation.

For a workshop type meeting where the format is more discussion based, brainstorming ideas onto a flip chart works well.

Props

This is a 3D visual aid. The obvious type of prop to use is your product if you have a physical product to demonstrate, but it's not necessarily the only way to use a prop.

Visual aids are there to help you make your point more memorable – make it stick. As with choosing images, think about how your prop links to your message.

Earlier, I mentioned Darren Tay (World Champion of Public Speaking 2016) – his prop was a pair of white underpants worn *over* his business suit. His choice of prop was influenced by the theme of the story – how he was made to wear something similar as a child at school and how his experience of bullying has taught him many valuable lessons. Clearly it takes a lot of confidence to use a prop in this way but it can be very effective and of course memorable – everyone in the audience that day will remember Darren's speech and his metaphor of wearing underpants over your clothes for too long. If you haven't watched this speech yet, check it out on YouTube to see how he effectively uses the prop.

More subtle types of props can be referencing a book that is relevant. I've also seen medical experts use skeletons or models of the human body as well as environmental speakers using goldfish bowls filled with clean and dirty water to demonstrate pollution. A globe could be a good prop to demonstrate topics around culture by pointing out different countries or to highlight time zones that may be relevant to building a social media campaign around peak times.

Bill Gates used a jar filled with mosquitos that he let loose on to an unsuspecting audience at a TED conference in 2009, to make a point that malaria can affect us all. Take a look at the video, *Mosquitoes, Malaria and Education*. This video is also a good example of how to show complex data in clean and easy-to-follow visual slides.

Your prop can be anything that serves to hook the audience into the point you are making. Here are some examples from my personal experience that might give you some inspiration:

I worked with a client a few years ago who was preparing a pitch for investors in his recruitment start-up business. The main thread of the pitch was that the company would revolutionize the recruitment industry. He used a little black notebook as a prop to contrast the old with the new – the black book of contacts was no longer enough to build a network: these days we need to leverage social media and so he threw the book to one side.

A similar example would be to highlight that directories such as Yellow Pages or BT phone books still exist but are much thinner than they used to be because much of what we search for is typically through use of our smart phones. Times have changed.

Over the years, I've run a number of presentation workshops for teenagers. I sometimes use my mobile phone as a prop in my opening to grab their attention.

I'll pull out my phone from my back pocket and tell them that when I was at their stage in life we didn't have phones. Never mind phones, we didn't have the internet! That always gets a laugh and breaks the ice.

When I was practising as a young lawyer, I'd often be representing clients at court hearings in connection with road traffic accidents. Many of the judges would use toy cars to ask witnesses to demonstrate exactly what happened. It was a brilliant yet simple way to make sure the facts were explained correctly – otherwise it could be quite confusing when describing left and right, believe it or not.

Hand-outs to support your message

I've stressed how important it is to keep any slides you use to be as clutter free as possible. That means that you are limited as to how much content you can insert into the slides. Sometimes it is helpful to have physical paper hand-outs to give to your audience to follow detailed or complex material. For example if you are discussing figures linking to target or trends or explaining parts of a project plan. It can be particularly useful to print charts and graphs as they can look quite busy on a slide and be difficult to follow up on a screen.

In that case be really strategic about when you give out your hand outs. If you leave them on people's chairs or on the table, they will start to flick through them and that takes their attention away from you. A better way to use documents during your presentation is to distribute them at the point that you want to use them. This will work even in an interview situation. When you do refer to your document and take everyone through it, blank your slides as discussed above until you are ready to go back to your slide presentation.

Another way that people like to use hand-outs is to provide a takeaway for the audience members. Very often at a seminar you'll be given the slides printed three to an A4 sheet. The thinking behind this is that it gives the audience something to jot notes onto as they follow along with the live presentation. I don't think this is a great way to use hand-outs. Printing three slides to a sheet makes the content too small to read anyway, plus if you have done your job right in creating visual slides then there really isn't much content for them to take away anyway – the slides only work with you there to explain them! A better way to create a more valuable type of hand out is to type up a Word document with a summary of your talk and hand that out after your presentation as a more valuable reference guide. Or you can email a PDF version later; that way you avoid wasting paper and in this day and age a digital format is much more user-friendly.

Resources for royalty free images

Freedigitalphotos.net
Gettyimages.co.uk

Canva.com
Stocksnap.io
Flickr.com

On a final note, only use the above tools if they enhance understanding. Sometimes, just you speaking and engaging your audience with your strong message and engaging delivery will be enough – you don't always need a visual aid.

TOP TIPS

- Only think about slides when you have written or planned your speech. Create a sketched outline for each slide to help you decide what type of images or phrases you might want to insert.

- Make sure you set aside time to create slides. In the same way as you would create a draft for your speech and then come back to refine it, keep refining your slides so that they act as hooks for your key messages.

- Once you have created your slide deck go through them all to check for a smooth consistent look with font style, colour and size on each slide.

- The purpose of any type of visual aid is to increase audience engagement and help them understand and remember your content better.

- Get creative with using props – your imagination is the limit. Watch videos on sites like TED.com to see how other speakers use props to give you some inspiration.

10

OPENINGS AND ENDINGS

You've spent a lot of time researching your content and then structuring it to align with the key messages you want to share. Now it's time to top and tail your material – like bookends. The beginning and end of your speech or presentation are arguably the most important parts and deserve time and effort to hone them to make them really work for you and your audience.

Open strong to grab their attention

Whether you are delivering a 10 minute pitch or a 90 minute keynote speech you have about 60 seconds to grab your audience's attention. Those few seconds are crucial to win them over. Your audience is unlikely to be 100% focused on you because they have thousands of other thoughts going through their minds. You have to compete with that. Get this bit wrong and you lose them.

Therefore you want to avoid wasting those precious few seconds with going over pleasantries like thank you or details about your company or role.

If you don't engage them early, you end up having to work harder and may be faced with an awkward silence in the room. This could happen for a number of reasons – many of which I've experienced first hand:

- **Speaking too quietly** – they need to be able to hear you and so think about your voice projection. If your audience struggle to hear you right from the start they switch off. I am naturally a quietly spoken person so for me it became a priority when I consistently received feedback from my audiences that they had to really listen carefully to hear me or just couldn't hear at all if they were sat at the back of the room. We'll look at this aspect in more detail later.

- **Not tweaking the material enough** – your opening lines need to create impact and pique interest. It takes a while to refine your content to come up with the right words to place at the top end of your speech but it is absolutely worth it. Audiences can be tough crowds, especially when they don't know you and are perhaps less sympathetic. They won't wait for you to build up to your best ideas.

- **Tech failure** – I've worked with a lot of speakers who have lost momentum even before they begin their speech and end up becoming flustered because the slides are not working or the microphone is not on etc. This anxiety also unsettles the audience. Check everything works before it is your turn to get up and speak.

There are many variables that can affect the impact of your opening section. Spend some time crafting and then rehearsing your opening so that you have it memorized.

The other huge benefit of nailing your opening is that it helps settle any nerves and gives you a confidence boost.

Ideas for your opening

Don't open with pleasantries or company details

You might have seen a lot of presenters open with 'thank you for inviting me', 'thank you for being here' or something similar. That is of course nice and polite but not very impactful. It's worth remembering that the audience only want to know what's in it for them, so resist this type of opening and hold it back until the end if you really feel as if you want to say some form of thanks.

Similarly listing credentials such as who your team are or your own role are not necessarily of interest to your audience. It may be relevant to your ability to deliver on a promise such as team capability for carrying out a project or task, but perhaps introduce this later. I can't tell you how many hundreds of business presentations I have sat through where the speaker does this and it becomes boring, which is another reason to do something different and set yourself apart by hooking in your audience first.

Most of the time, the audience will know who you are and what your role is – for example at an interview or in a team meeting. If you do go to present to an unfamiliar audience such as prospective clients then you can have your name and role up on a holding slide on the screen before you begin your speech. They can read it for themselves. Most of the time, you will be introduced so anything else becomes unnecessary.

Using pause to great effect

Taking a few seconds to pause before your opening line allows your audience to settle down but also brings their attention to you because it is unexpected – they will expect a presenter to begin speaking immediately so a pause of 10 seconds or so is unusual. It builds anticipation and will make them wonder what is coming next. Watch Darren Tay's Toastmasters 2016 winning speech to see how this is done.

Tell them a story

We already know that successful presentations include stories. As human beings we are hardwired to tune into them – it is how we have passed on knowledge throughout our history. What better way than to open with one?

The story can be personal – about a challenge you have overcome or an experience you've had that made a profound impact on you that links to your topic in some way. This way you can share first hand why you are interested in the topic.

Or like, Ken Robinson did in TED talk about the little girl drawing a picture – tell a story about someone else.

The key here is to jump right into your story and not start with 'I want to tell you a story'. If you watch Ken Robinson you'll see exactly how he gets right into the stories.

Shocking fact or statistic

Present the problem in a way that acts as a wake up call. If you can find a fact or figures that support your message then use that to open with. Just reciting facts or figures can be boring or uninspiring. Put some context around it. Remember in an earlier chapter I talked about my client who delivered a presentation on the topic of how much milk was being wasted in their business? He worked out the volume of an Olympic swimming pool and then calculated how many gallons it would take to fill it. Then he posed a question asking the audience to guess how many gallons it would take to fill the pool. This created immediate engagement. Then, when he told them that it was the amount of milk being wasted in the business it hammered home the point and made it memorable.

Another way in which you could do this is to ask your audience to guess and then hold back the answer until later so they continue to listen!

You could use historical references which helps put things into context as well. I often speak on the topic of gender diversity and I sometimes use the fact that it is almost 100 years since women got the right to vote in the UK and then develop my speech to discuss what progress we've made since then.

Humour

If you can pull this off, it works like a charm. Being able to make your audience laugh right from the start is one of the fastest ways to get them interested in your talk. Telling a joke could work but you have to be able to deliver it well plus the joke has to be relevant and appropriate. Please don't use this opening if you don't have something that is on point and has been tested; the risks of a joke falling flat are just too great.

The best humour often comes from the unexpected – for example if you make a joke at your own expense such as your accent or a quirky habit you have etc.

Shawn Achor's TED talk *The Happy Secret to Better Work* is a brilliant example of telling a personal childhood story in a humorous way and then smoothly connecting it to the main topic of his talk which is positive psychology. He uses irony in telling the story and that is what gets most of the laughs.

Using memorable quotes

Using quotes is quite a popular way to open a speech. The challenge is to find something that is not too clichéd, overused or even inaccurate. The benefit is that most people have heard of it and so it is familiar, but if it's overused then it can come across as cheesy. Put some of your own explanation around it. Go that extra mile – it will set you apart from average presenters.

An example of an overused quote is:

'Be the change you want to see in the world' – Gandhi
A way to develop this a little further is to say something like:
'Many of us have heard this quote before… What that means for me is that it's really important to lead by example…'

The authenticity of some of these popular quotes is debatable. Over time quotes have been attributed to famous people who actually never used those exact words – they have been misquoted or never said them in the first place!

One of my favourite quotes is:

'Our deepest fear is not that we are inadequate. Our deepest fear is that we are powerful beyond measure. It is our light, not our darkness that most frightens us.'

This is a quote from a book written by Marianne Williamson. It is also a quote that is given to one of the characters in the 2005 movie *Coach Carter*, a true story about a basketball coach. I often refer to it in my speeches on leadership topics.

However, the same quote has been attributed to Nelson Mandela in his inaugural address in 1994, and yet if you watch that speech on YouTube you'll notice the quote is not in it.

If you use a well-known quote, check its accuracy and try to frame it in a novel way. Spend some time researching lesser known quotes from well-known figures that not many people have used.

Have some fun and maybe use quotes from TV or movie characters that people know of, like my *Coach Carter* example above:

'Do, or do not. There is no "try".' – Yoda, *The Empire Strikes Back.*

Start to collect quotes that may come in useful later.

To get maximum impact, put your quote on a slide and then pause to let your audience read it before moving on with your speech. Make sure the slide is visually appealing but without detracting from the words.

Asking a question

Asking questions gets the audience immediately engaged as they are invited to think about something straight away as in the Olympic pool example above. There are several ways in which you can use this technique – by asking a question where you expect a response by a show of hands or asking rhetorical questions. The former can work well if you have a willing audience. By putting their hands up, they are showing some level of participation and trust. However, if you have a reticent audience, they will not want to put their hands up, in fact it is quite possible that they are sitting there with their arms crossed silently saying: 'Come on then – impress me.'

Rhetorical questions are a safer bet. A thought-provoking question to which your audience is providing an answer silently in their minds – one that requires a simple yes or no answer. Or you can ask questions that arouse curiosity.

Frame it as a 'you'-focused question:

'When was the last time you…?'
'What would you do if…?'
'How would you feel if…?'
'What do you think is the number one reason…?'

In her TED talk, Amy Cuddy opens with a promise of teaching us a two-minute life hack that will benefit us, but before she delivers on that promise Amy asks us to think about our posture – do a little audit:

'How many of you are sort of making yourselves smaller? Maybe you're hunching, crossing your legs, maybe wrapping your ankles?'

She goes on to discuss what those postures mean eventually, but before that she has managed to pique the interest of the audience by saying 'We'll come back to that in a few minutes...' Now they are all curious! She not only engages them mentally but physically as well.

Imagine/what if...

Open with the words 'Imagine if...'

This technique is very similar to telling a story. You are taking the audience on a journey but this time placing them in a scene or situation linked to your message. You invite them to imagine a better or perhaps worse scenario in the future and then build your speech around that. By including them in this future pacing you connect them to the outcome.

Introduce your topic when giving a longer talk

Sometimes it is helpful to give an overview to incentivize your audience to keep listening to the end if it's a longer speech. This works really well in presentations where you are teaching something or introducing a new concept. It's like a teaser or trailer – your core promise to deliver value. Keep it short and limit it to only be about one or two sentences long.

For example:

'Most people find networking events uncomfortable, especially when it's much easier to connect with people online. Today, we'll look at how to use social media to help you make networking less painful and more meaningful.'

'Today we'll look at how my experience/research/our department has found a way to...'

Avoid using 'I' and instead say 'Today we'll look at' or 'By the end of this talk you'll...' Then jump straight into your presentation.

EXERCISE

Have a go at drafting a summary that can act as a trailer for your topic:

1. Summarize the problem or current situation.

2. Identify what they will learn or insights they'll gain.

3. What are the results or outcomes – 'you'll see or you'll be able to...'

Your audience are not so much interested in what you say as they are in what they will get after you have spoken.

Memorize your opening lines – you want to ensure you get off to a powerful start.

Powerful endings

This is the part where you make it clear you have finished the presentation and deliver on your promise to provide value. It can be uncomfortable if the audience don't realize you have finished and there is an awkward silence. You want to avoid a weak ending: if you haven't prepared your final sentence in advance, you might end up closing your presentation with your words simply trailing off self-consciously. Similarly, running out of time can mean you end up cutting off the last part and finishing abruptly. At the very least you can say thank you – that signals to them it's over. If you are in an interview situation you may only have time for this type of ending.

People tend to remember what they heard last and therefore this section is just as important as your opening. If for some reason your talk has to be cut short, make sure you can easily cut to your rehearsed ending with your final closing message.

Make it personal to them – remember you are aiming to answer WIIFM ('what's in it for me?') and so your concluding remarks need to wrap up your talk in such a way as to answer that question. What do they get out of this presentation? Why will it help them? What are the next steps?

Many of the techniques we looked at for opening can also be used to close your presentation:

- A short story
- An impactful quote
- A rhetorical question
- An interesting fact

Other ways to close

Summarize your material

You can summarize your content if your presentation is long – 'to summarize/ conclude…'. But if you've stuck to the format of clear and simple key points, you won't need to recap your talk. Just list the main points again.

Call back to your opening line

You can refer back to your opening by answering the rhetorical question you asked at the beginning or finishing a story that you started. Opening with a story and then leaving them hanging is an advanced technique but can work really well with practice.

A memorable tweet type phrase

Use a tweet-worthy short phrase that can be a memorable takeaway message, such as:

> 'Stay hungry. Stay foolish' – Steve Jobs, Stanford University commencement address in 2005.

Here Steve Jobs uses three stories to motivate the graduating class at Stanford University and then closes with that simple memorable phrase. I say 'tweet-worthy' because tweets are short and get noticed. They have to grab attention in just 280 characters. Your closing phrase needs to be like a good tweet: able to grab attention in just 280 characters.

A call to action

Are you inviting them to do something with the information you just shared? If so make it obvious – what is the next step? What should they do when they leave your presentation? Give you funding, buy your product, implement a new way of working?

Where to place the questions section

Don't end with questions.

It is highly likely that you will have a question and answer section but position it so that you still have your powerful close to come last. The problem with ending on a question is that you risk going off track and then lose any momentum you have built throughout the rest of your speech. Not only that, you lose the opportunity to bring home your call to action or closing point which should be the last thing they hear.

Introduce your questions by saying something like, 'Before I wrap up I would like to open the floor to questions...' Then after the last question, bring it back round with 'To wrap up...' or 'I'll leave you with...' To ensure you maintain control, state that you have time for two or three questions so that you manage the audience's expectations and can keep to time for your overall slot. Sometimes, you'll find that a question opens up a lively debate, which is fantastic as this only enhances audience interaction further. A problem could be that it runs on too long. Be prepared to respectfully cut the discussion short and bring the focus back to you either to move onto another question or to your closing message. You will find your own style of doing this and may want to write out some phrases in advance so that you are better prepared. Some that I've used are:

'That's a really good point; can we pause there for now and carry on that discussion over the networking…'

'This is clearly a topic that's relevant to many people and we could carry on exploring this all afternoon if time allowed, however I'd also like to make time to take another question if that's all right…'

'We're coming towards the close of this session so I'd like to wrap it up there for now if I may. Maybe we can continue this discussion later?'

TOP TIPS

- Memorize your opening and closing lines and rehearse them.
- Start to build up a bank of quotes you could use in your future speeches.
- Watch other speakers on YouTube or TED.com to see how they open their speeches.
- Test out different ways in which to open and close and find the best fit for you – perhaps have two variations for an upcoming speech and get some feedback from friends or colleagues as to which ones make more impact.

11

PERSONALITY AND MESSAGE

What are you like to work with? That's what your audience are wondering if you are in front of an interview panel or pitching to potential clients. They want some clues about your personality – whether you'll fit in with their team or be easy to relate to. When you communicate with others in meetings or in presentation style settings, you have a great opportunity to showcase who you are. Not only that, but when you bring your personality into any presentation it really does bring it to life – anyone can read off a script, but it's you that can add value by making your delivery more engaging through your own personal style.

It's also not just about how you deliver your message. Whatever your topic or intention for the audience may be, people will make assumptions about you before you even open your mouth to speak, regardless of whether you are in an interview situation selling yourself or presenting on behalf of your team or organization. It is still *you* that your audience sees. Other people form an opinion of us instantly – within a matter of seconds so it's important to be able influence their opinion in a positive way.

What does personality actually mean?

Personality is who you are. It is how you behave when you feel comfortable, how you hold yourself when you are most relaxed.

One of the few things you can truly control in life, is how you define yourself and the choices you make. Whatever constraints you may have around the context, content or timing of your presentation, you can control one thing – how you convey your personality.

Authenticity and how that relates to better audience connection

The best speakers are those who can connect with their audience on an emotional level. They are authentic.

Authenticity is a buzz word that is perhaps over used these days in business, but it is nevertheless a highly desirable characteristic. I like to think of it as: 'what you see is what you get'. It's being yourself and showing your human side – even being slightly vulnerable. People would much rather see this kind of speaker than someone who hides behind a mask or comes across as a robot talking at the audience.

However, displaying an authentic personality is sometimes easier said than done.

In an earlier chapter we looked at the concept of building your own brand and developing a competitive edge. Showcasing your personality is a big part of developing this. People like to do business with people they know, like and trust. In your presentation, you need to demonstrate that that person is you.

People buy into *you,* not what you are selling or explaining. Your authenticity is what will resonate with people and make them want more of whatever service, product or skills you have to offer. Personality is what will set you apart and make you more attractive as a candidate in an interview process.

When you are developing relationships at work or with clients, you do this over a period of time. As you get to work with each other or meet each other more often, the more trust and respect increases. When you only have one chance to give a presentation then you have to make that connection with audience much faster.

Being an authentic presenter is about you feeling totally congruent and comfortable being yourself in front of an audience. If you don't appear confident and aligned with your message and how you say it, people will switch off.

Creating rapport is necessary before someone is willing to listen to you. Rapport is the ability to connect with others in a way that creates trust and understanding. If you are able to put your audience at ease, they are far more likely to be receptive to your ideas and the information you want to share. By allowing them to see you as an individual you will add a personal element.

The personal impression you make dramatically influences the audience experience. Authenticity and enthusiasm for your topic or message are essential in creating that connection with your audience.

This is even more relevant in recruitment situations. Inevitably you will be 'selling yourself' in front of a panel of decision makers that you have never met before. You have a small window of opportunity to influence others to think of you as the best candidate. Not only that, but you are up against other talented individuals who most likely have the same level of technical skills, experience and academic track record. So what will set you apart from them?

A few years ago when I was working as a senior solicitor in an international law firm in their London office, I helped out at the graduate recruitment day. Each year law firms like these receive several hundred applications from out-standing candidates. Most have an upper second class degree and many have a first class degree. Think about this – when you only have 12 vacancies to offer it is extremely difficult to sift through all the application forms or CVs to get down to 50 candidates that are invited to the graduate day. It was and still is quite competitive to secure positions in these types of firms and indeed not that much different in other industries. To even get past the first hurdle, each candidate had to impress and communicate their competitive edge – not just with aca-demic qualifications, but with extracurricular activities such as community con-tributions, leadership roles and interesting gap years.

At that initial stage, the only way to narrow down to a shortlist of 50 candi-dates was to look for glimpses of personality, areas of interest and of course any relevant work experience. The graduate day itself was designed to give the can-didates a chance to ask questions and get a feel for what it would be like to work at the firm. A number of solicitors were lined up to give short talks about their areas of work and take questions from the graduates. I was one of them.

Obviously of course, it was also a screening process for the firm. Every can-didate had a panel interview at some point during the day. Then there was the lunch. This was one of the most important parts of the day however, that may not have been obvious to everyone. We had a buffet lunch which was also a networking opportunity. This was the segment where we were watching the graduates closely. It was their chance to showcase their interpersonal skills as well as providing a glimpse into their personality. What they didn't know was that in a separate room we had a board on the wall with all their photos and a box for us to leave comments. Throughout the day we kept going into that room to add comments and insights we got from our conversations with the graduates. That information was taken into account together with feedback from the interview panels to weigh up who would be a great fit for our firm. Personality was a very important factor.

I've been working with professionals on their presentation skills for a long time and more often than not people tend to have a different persona when they get up to speak than how they come across in everyday interactions. They tend to become serious and sometimes detached. Usually this is unintentional and anxiety at having to speak in front of groups can cause this to happen.

When I run presentation workshops I give the group at least two opportunities to practise speeches in front of the rest of the group. One is a technical work-place topic and the other is a personal story of their choice – the sillier the better. The difference in delivery style is remarkable. When someone delivers a light hearted anecdote their facial muscles relax and the tone of voice relaxes and becomes lighter. It is the quickest way I can get them to see and feel what a difference it makes to relax and be yourself.

My job is to encourage speakers to bring more of the open and engaging delivery into the workplace topic. We seem to be conditioned into giving flat presentations filled with technical data because we think that is what professional audiences want. There is a sense that in order to be professional you have to develop a serious presentation facade.

Identifying what makes up your personality and style

Everything you have done to this point makes up who you are – your experiences – academic, professional and personal. Your CV gives a snapshot of your personality when you include extracurricular activities. That in no way gives the interviewer or your audience a true reflection of who you are until they hear you speak.

We spend a lot of time at work but there is much more to us than our professional careers. What interests you outside of work? What causes or hobbies are you passionate about? What films or books interest you? Your preferences and opinions are what make up your personality and bringing those insights into your communication through anecdotes can be really engaging.

EXERCISE

Ask five people whom know you well how they would describe your:

- Personality – ask for insights into your personality. What are some of the common traits that come up? When you get this type of information fed back to you it will give you a better understanding of how others see you. This is so valuable as it will help you identify personality aspects that you can weave into your presentation style.

- Strengths – what you good at? For example if you are a great storyteller or have an infectious sense of humour, you can work that into your presentation because it comes naturally to you. If a strength is fantastic organizational skills, then think about how you can insert a case study discussing this into the presentation.

- Weaknesses – we all have our own view of our strengths and weaknesses, but it is really valuable to get an objective perspective, as our own perception doesn't necessarily match that of our audience. For example you might not be aware that when under pressure, your voice becomes a lot quieter or you start to speak too fast. Learning about these aspects increases your self-awareness and helps you to make adjustments.

When you get feedback like this pause to think for a moment if what other people perceive is accurate and if not would you consider adjusting your approach. For me personally, I consistently got feedback in the early years of my career that I was unapproachable until people got to know me. That was never my intention – I thought I was approachable and friendly all the time. I realized later that my shyness that kept me from speaking up was being misinterpreted.

Weaving in your personality with your message

As I've discussed, your presentation needs to be crafted for the benefit of your audience. The primary focus needs to be on them so that you can persuade them to take action or understand something very specific after your presentation.

Generally your framework for the presentation will be built around a problem and/or solution with a logical path to your call to action or conclusion at the end. Amongst this, you use stories or analogies to put some context around your content to make it more memorable and engaging for your audience. Part of this engagement though must also come from them connecting with you personally.

In a keynote speech we get to see much more of the speaker's personality as these types of speeches are light on technical information and heavier on motivational or inspirational content – much of which comes from personal stories. Often the stories the speakers share make them more vulnerable to the audience because they'll cover difficult issues such as mistakes the speaker has made or challenges they have faced. It's the glimpse of vulnerability that people can connect to because everyone can relate to that.

This is quite an advanced skill and I'm definitely not saying you should always include very personal stories but, finding a way to bring a little bit of *you* into your presentations will create a better connection with your audience – whoever they are.

You could have 10 different speakers on the same topic with the same speech structure and you'll get 10 different ways in which the message has been shared. Why? Because everyone has a different personality or point of view, different ways in which they emphasize points – all of which are unique to them.

Your style is unique – no one can present the way you do.

This is one of the main reasons why I always recommend that presenters ideally create their own content and slides so that they can take ownership of it and tweak it to fit their natural style. If for some reason, you are given someone else's speech or presentation to deliver then devote some time to add in your own perspective.

You bring your personality into your presentation by choosing how to bring your content to life – through your stories and examples, your body language and your voice. We'll cover these aspects in more detail in later chapters.

There is a whole chapter dedicated to storytelling for the purpose of engaging your audience and improving their experience. Here we look at stories in a different context – how using stories lets us see more of you.

I've got a number of personal stories in my back catalogue that I can use in my speeches, many of which showcase silly things that happened to me and the lessons I took from them.

I have a few stories relating to my debilitating fear of public speaking. When I tell them I'm completely honest and often use self-deprecating humour. I tell them because they help me connect to my audience's own concerns around public speaking confidence. After my embarrassing episode freezing up in a team meeting that I described in an earlier chapter, I decided to be proactive and get some help through workshops and coaching. That is a moment that is very personal to me and it makes me look vulnerable, but it's exactly that which others can relate to. It's one of the stories I share in my TEDx talk which is online for the foreseeable future and not something I can take back. Of course I knew that when I decided to tell it. When people decide whether to book me as a speaker or work with me as their coach, they'll most likely watch that video online to see if I am someone they could connect with.

When I qualified from law school I was one of the few people in my class who still didn't have a job offer. Most of my classmates were sorted with jobs that also had a nice salary and benefits package. I must have applied to 100 firms and didn't get a positive reply from any of them. One of my friends who had already secured a fantastic job offer was brutally honest with me and told me to focus on smaller high street firms and visit them personally to hand over my CV. That was the scariest thing I had faced at that point – I couldn't give a presentation in class never mind walk into law firms asking for an on-the-spot interview. However, I realized I didn't have much choice if I wanted to be a lawyer I needed a training position in a law firm so that I could at least become qualified. I literally walked into twenty-five law firms in one day and everyone said no thanks, except the very last place I went into. It was dark and the office was about to close. The cleaner, who also doubled up as the part-time receptionist took pity on me and asked me to wait while she went to get the office manager. It was that one meeting that set the wheels in motion for my legal career. Years later I did make it to the top city firms that had originally rejected me. The themes I can draw from a story like that are resilience, stepping out of your comfort zone, focusing on your goal and being patient.

Not all stories have to be serious of course. The light hearted ones are great – you might even get a few laughs. In Chapter 10, under the section on Humour, I mention Shawn Achor's TED talk *The Happy Secret to Better Work*. This is such a great example of how to weave in some humour into a personal anecdote. If you haven't seen the video yet, I highly recommend that you do. In a nutshell, he talks about a time when he and his little sister were playing as children and somehow she fell from the top bunk bed. It was Shawn's responsibility as the older brother to make sure she didn't come to any harm, and yet there she was on the floor about to cry and he was worried he might get into trouble. Thinking fast, he persuaded her that she was a unicorn hence switching her focus from crying to something she really identified with and would make her happy. Playing games when we are young is such a normal everyday example that many of us can identify with. Shawn makes it sound funny with a clever build up in the story arc and then finally links it to his topic for the speech: Positive Psychology.

A few years ago I bought a smart TV that was connected to the internet. At that time I wasn't subscribed to online services like Netflix or Amazon Prime even though I am a TV addict – I love my boxsets! When I realized I could connect to these streaming services I literally binge watched an entire five seasons of a popular series over a few weeks. Little did I realize that every month I was going over my broadband allowance I was incurring a fine. When I found out I immediately increased my broadband limit. That was an expensive mistake. The points I can draw out from this are – always investigate all possibilities. When you make a mistake, make sure you learn from it so it never happens again!

Any material is potential anecdote material for you – your imagination is the limit. You can draw inspiration from work experiences, sports activities, holidays, school or university experiences etc.

Now it's your turn:

EXERCISE

Spend some time brainstorming your anecdotes now. This sort of material is incredibly useful for presentations as well as interview situations when you get questions such as: 'what has been your biggest challenge to date?' Or 'what has been your biggest achievement so far?' The anecdotes you choose don't have to be heroic stories. Think about work situations, projects you've worked on or sporting challenges you have been involved in – cover everything from all the way back to your childhood to the present day. Don't worry about whether it will make a good story or if it will be funny for now, that refinement can come later. Look back to the Shawn Achor example – all that happened was that his sister fell while they were playing with their toys unsupervised. Nothing remarkable about that. It's how he delivers the story that makes all the difference – he brings his personality into the delivery. The link he chose to make from this story to the main topic was about the impact of positive psychology. You can craft these types of story pieces too – it just takes a bit of preparation.

When you are selecting examples of experiences you might be willing to share, think about the point you want to connect it to:

- What did you learn?
- What obstacles did you overcome?
- What new insights did you get?
- Is it what inspired you to choose your career path?

Addressing these aspects and weaving them into stories or examples, you let the audience into your world. They get more information about what's important to you, what back to your childhood to present day. Don't worry about whether it will make a good story or if it will be funny for now, that refinement can come later. Look back to the Shawn Achor example – all that happened was that his sister fell while they were playing with their toys unsupervised. Nothing remarkable about that. It's how he your values and priorities are. By going through this process, you will have some ready-made material that you can rely on even at short notice for example preparing for unseen presentation topics at an assessment centre or being challenged by the panel in an interview.

Learning how to bring personality into presentations from other speakers

I've mentioned TED talks quite a bit in this book in order to give you some reference points. The ones I like to refer to often are those that I think show the personalities of the speakers. When I watch them I feel it's as if that is the same person I would see in real life, off the stage.

Let's take Ken Robinson for example in his TED talk *Do Schools Kill Creativity?* Through his storytelling you get to see the fun side of him – he is able to tell stories in a humorous way and laughs along with the audience. We also get to see a more authoritative side of him when he brings the speech back to the serious points he is making. He uses a variety of facial expressions and vocal variety to add different styles of emphasis depending on what he is sharing at the particular moment in time. It feels like Ken is being authentic.

Another good example is Amy Cuddy's TED talk *Your Body Language Shapes Who You Are*. Amy is a Harvard Professor who talks about how our body language influences our thoughts; more specifically our level of confidence and ability to deal with stressful situations. She is softly spoken and yet comes across as authoritative in her own way. Right towards the end of her speech we hear her personal story of how she had a crisis of confidence when she was a college student and how she came through it. We get to see the vulnerable side of her personality and can connect with her emotionally.

You may not want to come across as vulnerable in the ways I have described in the examples above, but there is still plenty of scope for you to be authentic and create a 'what you see is what you get' experience for your audience.

Personal presentation and appearance

Authenticity includes your personal style and appearance as well as your personality. It's human nature to form quick judgments about people, even before they have said anything – much of it is at an unconscious level, a 'feeling' or 'gut instinct'. So what is it that influences others into forming that instant opinion of us? It ranges from what we are wearing to the visual cues our body language provides.

Becoming aware of non verbal cues

What non verbal signals are you sending? Are you standing tall and giving the impression of confidence or are you finding it difficult to make eye contact which could be interpreted as nervousness or lack of confidence? People make assumptions about our capabilities, levels of confidence and interpersonal skills just from observing us for a few seconds. What we do with our gestures is mostly outside of our conscious awareness. For example, you might cross your arms because that feels comfortable for you, however someone who doesn't know you that well might think that you may be feeling defensive because you've adopted a closed posture. Or, your facial expression could be interpreted as if you are anxious but in reality you are just concentrating and thinking of what to say next. Excitement and nervous energy can also have an impact – affecting our movements in a way that makes us move less naturally than normal. If you want to give the impression of confidence and competency, then make sure your body language is consistent with that. Skip to Chapter 13 on body language for more on this.

How you communicate through your posture, facial expressions and gestures is something you can control to a certain extent. Becoming aware of how you speak and move in presentation or interview situations is a good place to start. Seek out opportunities for rehearsing in front of others and getting feedback from them as well as video taping yourself so that you can see how you speak and move. That way you can bring conscious awareness to how you want to come across in front of your audience. In practical terms that could mean pausing for moment to mentally check-in with yourself and assess what is going on at that particular time so that you can adapt if necessary, for example:

- a friendly smile to go with the handshake when you walk into a meeting
- nodding or acknowledging with a smile to make sure you are looking interested
- avoiding nervous unconscious habits such as playing with hair or jewellery

Choice of clothing and grooming

What should you wear to a work presentation or an interview for a new job? There used to be a time when going to an interview meant that the only real choice was to wear a suit. That is no longer the case. The same is true for normal every day work attire – whether that is in an office or not. Many organizations these days are happy for their staff to adopt a smart casual or relaxed approach. Some companies are extremely casual such as IT or media firms. It really does depend on the industry sector and culture of the organization as to what is acceptable.

When preparing for an interview, I would suggest doing some research by looking at the company website to see if there are team photos that might give you a clue as to how staff normally dress. You could even go and visit the location beforehand to see for yourself if possible. You want to aim for something that is appropriate for the type of role you are going for but also something that suits your natural style. If you are unsure of what to choose, I personally think that it's always better to dress smarter than more casual.

If you are giving a presentation to colleagues then you wouldn't need to do anything outside of your normal routine in respect of an appropriate outfit. If you are presenting to clients or going offsite then you may need to dress smarter than usual. As with the interview scenario – find out what is appropriate for that particular event.

Whatever you end up wearing, try it on beforehand. I never wear something new to an important meeting or speech I am giving without having tried it out first. Here's why – I don't want to have to worry about feeling uncomfortable or restricted. It's just one less thing to focus on. Even if you have an outfit you've worn before – try it all on anyway so you can check for any spills or damage. I once worked with a colleague who was always smartly dressed in a pin-striped suit. One day, he came into my office to discuss a case before heading out to a meeting. That day I noticed that there was a big hole on one of the legs just above the knee of his trousers. I wanted to say something but felt too embarrassed to mention it. All I could think was that he must have got dressed in the dark. The point is that you don't want to draw attention to yourself for the wrong reasons. Try to look out for anything that could be a distraction – even small things like price tags on the sole of your shoes. Most people think that they can't be seen so why bother removing them? Actually you can see them with every step someone takes. Small point, but it can be a reflection of attention to detail.

Similarly, accessories or jewellery can be a distraction if they make a noise when you move.

Good grooming and a tidy appearance are essential whatever you choose to wear. Again, it's all about attention to detail and being congruent with the professional image you want to portray. Have a think about simple things like clean nails and combed hair.

You may have heard the saying 'You never get a second chance to make a first impression'. Whether you believe that or not, isn't it worth putting in some preparation to ensure you take the opportunity to showcase yourself in the best possible light?

First impressions matter.

TOP TIPS

- Watch other speakers and look out for how they bring in their personality – what examples or stories do they use and how do they deliver them?

- Spend some time analysing how you might describe your personality – once you are clear about that, find ways in which you can reflect that in your next presentation.

- Remember, people make snap judgments about us as soon as we walk into a room. Think about your posture and body language – are you communicating the way you intend to? To increase your self-awareness, record yourself practising a presentation and as you watch it back compare what you see and hear to how you thought you were communicating.

- Be purposeful about what you want your image to say about you – do the clothes and accessories you choose reflect your personal style as well as balance what is appropriate for your audience, particularly if you are going for job interview? Remember to carry out some research about what a potential employer might expect.

12

OVERCOMING NERVES

Speaking in public is a challenge for most people. It's something that affects individuals across all sectors and all levels of seniority, even those that look as if they are supremely confident. If the thought of getting up in front of others fills you with dread then know that you are not alone! I have coached some very senior people over the years that are at the top of their profession, highly respected and great in discussions and meetings. Yet the thought of presenting to a room full of clients and peers makes them very nervous. This is not something that people feel they can be open about – partly due to the fact that when you get to a certain stage in your career people assume that naturally you will have the confidence that goes hand in hand with your experience.

As you know, I have no problem admitting openly that this was something that was a major problem for me – the fear held me back from being the best I could be in my career for a very long time. I found tools and techniques to help me move beyond fear and this chapter discusses various options that could help you too.

The anxiety that many of us experience in these situations is a fear of not wanting to fail or look silly. Intellectually we know that, but our minds and bodies go into an automatic response that involves anything from blushing to visibly shaking hands and feelings of nausea. Much of what is going on there is a response to an adrenalin rush which is the body's natural response to getting ready for action or react to a perceived threat. If you think about it, we react in similar ways physically when we feel excitement. The challenge is to train our minds to interpret these symptoms in a positive way.

Adequate preparation of content and rehearsal

For me, hands down the most important thing to do to create a bedrock of confidence is to prepare adequately. This includes crafting your content to a standard that you are happy with and creating it well in advance of your presentation date so that you have enough time to internalize it. While the physical manifestations of nerves can be hard to control: rehearsal is something that you can control. If you put in the effort, you could have a big impact on the outcome. Feeling prepared can greatly reduce the kind of nervousness that arises from feeling out of control. The more you rehearse the more you develop that muscle memory so that when the presentation day arrives you are no longer treading on unfamiliar territory. Remember – when you rehearse, make sure you speak your presentation out loud.

There really is no better way to develop your confidence muscle than to prepare well and then continue to find opportunities to speak – the more you do it the easier it gets.

Mental preparation is equally important and the rest of this chapter takes a look at your various options.

Moving away from negative self-talk

The first step is to examine what might go through your mind just before you get up to speak – whether that is at an assessment centre, in an interview or in front of a bigger audience. Some examples of common negative self-talk include:

- 'I'm really nervous'
- 'I'll probably forget what I'm going to say'
- 'This is a tough audience'
- 'I'll look silly'

Allowing yourself to think these things or anything similar will make you more nervous.

Don't forget that your audience would much rather it was you than them delivering the presentation. Remember this – most people fear speaking in public. They would rather be in the audience than up at the front delivering the presentation like you will be doing so already you are a step ahead.

Direct your mind to where you want it to go. Rather than reinforcing to yourself that you feel nervous, switch the meaning so that you perceive the feeling as an adrenaline rush, helping you to be super focused and ready to perform. Instead of worrying about forgetting your lines, remind yourself of your back up plan – your notes are there if you need them – and that, because of all your preparation, you know everything well anyway.

Reframe everything in a more positive way. The facts remain the same but the meaning you now choose to attach to them are different. Think about past experiences that have been positive for you. Reflect back on those to shift to a more positive frame of mind.

The relevance of sports psychology to confidence in speaking

When a team in any sports discipline is preparing to go out and compete in a match or game, the coach or manager will typically give a last minute motivational pep talk. This helps them get in the right frame of mind. There are also some illuminating examples of famous performers and how they cope with the lead up to a major event.

For instance, Mark Bailey in the *Daily Telegraph* has written about Wayne Rooney's pre-match preparation. Rooney speaks to the kit man the night before a game to ask what the team will be wearing so he can use this information to help him prepare mentally. Every night before a big game, Rooney visualizes the match – imagining how he will be performing in minute detail right down to the kit he will be wearing. It's something he has been doing his whole life. He rehearses a positive mental experience.

Similarly, Jessica Ennis-Hill prior to the London 2012 Olympics. When all the hopes of the British public were pinned on her success, she used visualization to think about the perfect technique to help her physical performance.

Michael Phelps, one of the most successful Olympians, talks about visualization in his autobiography *No Limits*. For him, it is just as essential as the hours of rigorous practice in the pool and gym, proper nutrition and adequate sleep. Like the other sportspeople above, Phelps will imagine a swimming race in minute detail with vivid sounds, images and feelings. He will go through every possible scenario of the race by imagining all the things that can go well for him and all the things that could go wrong and how he will cope with them so that he is prepared for all eventualities.

That's great if you are an athlete, but what about if you have to motivate yourself just before a speech?

Susan Karcz, editor of *Harvard Medical Magazine,* has commented on the fact that this type of mental preparation is commonly used by sports psychologists and coaches to help optimize their performance. They will turn over in their mind every situation, obstacle, mistake and success multiple times so that they are mentally prepared.

If this technique works for world class athletes to help condition their minds to think clearly under pressure, then it might be worth giving it a go to see if it is something that might help you in overcoming nerves around speaking. This can be especially helpful in a job-seeking situation – when you attend an interview or assessment centre. These are high pressure situations that require you to be at your very best. Wouldn't it be great to find a technique that helps set you up for success?

What visualization is and how to incorporate it

Visualization is a technique for using your imagination to create the outcome you want. It's like a mental warm up. It is sometimes referred to as mental rehearsal or imagery. We all use our imaginations all the time so this is not anything new. Using your imagination with deliberate intent can help increase your confidence in speaking and improve your delivery.

Most of the time we go through our daily routines on autopilot, unconsciously going about our day without taking a few moments to check in with ourselves as to what outcome we want. It is very powerful to be able to guide the mind in the direction in which you want it to go – you get what you focus on so why not be deliberate about focusing on positive outcomes?

EXERCISE

The following exercise will require you to read through the steps a few times to familiarize yourself with them as this works well as a closed eye process. The alternative is to ask someone to read out the steps to you and guide you through them or, you can read out the steps and record them on your phone so that you can play it back.

- First, close your eyes and relax.

- Set the scene and see your presentation in detail, so that you are absolutely clear about what you have to do.

- In a relaxed state, see yourself in the scene as if watching on a big movie screen, as you are about to give your presentation exactly as you want it to go. See yourself in this picture as you are about to speak to your audience.

- Make the scene as perfect as you want it, but imagine in detail where you are standing or sitting, what the room looks like, focus on the lighting and furniture. See what clothes you are wearing and who else is in the room with you. Use all your senses to make the details as rich as possible – vivid colours, sounds and even smells. What do you see? What do you feel? What do you hear?

- Now, you can step into the scene on the screen and imagine delivering your presentation for real in the present tense as if it is actually happening now. This time you are actually within the picture – look at the scene through your own eyes. See what you would see, hear what you would hear. Notice how well the audience is responding to you. Really ramp up the intensity of the pictures, sounds and feelings. This is your mind movie that you can replay over and over again.

Some people find it difficult to use this technique at first – they struggle to close their eyes and bring up clear images. That's ok. You don't need to see images for this process to work. If you don't see pictures, you might get a feeling or a sense of what the scenario might look like. You can still hear sounds of you speaking confidently and the audience applauding. Your imagined scenarios can include any of the senses.

You can create these mind movies anytime you want and replay them again and again to reinforce the positive impact – it costs nothing except a few minutes of your time. If you write down your goals/outcomes before you visualize them, it can make the process even more powerful. This is a good technique to do last thing at night.

Meditation for calmness

Mindfulness and meditation are other techniques that many people find useful in helping them to keep calm and move away from distracting thoughts.

The practice of meditation is about *non-doing* or *non-striving* which is the opposite to our normal pace of rushing around going about our daily routines. Through meditation, you learn to train your mind to let go of negative thoughts like the ones mentioned above. By becoming aware of these negative thoughts and learning to let go of them or gently turning your mind to a single focus such as your breath, the strength of the negative thought begins to reduce.

This is more of a regular practice rather than a one-off or short-term fix.

There are many routes into finding out about meditation if you've never experienced it. A good way to experiment is to use one of the many apps that are now available either free or to buy that provide guided meditations, such as Omvana or Headspace.

Breathing techniques

Breathing is, of course, something we do without thinking. However, when we get nervous we breathe from the chest. This is shallow breathing which can create shortness of breath, leading to increased anxiety. It can also make us sound less confident when the voice starts to shake.

Deep breathing from the abdomen, ensures that you have enough air coming into your lungs and has the effect of calming nerves. Focusing on a good breathing technique is part of the practice of meditation and it can help you prepare for a calm and controlled presentation.

Here is a simple and effective routine that you try at any time.

EXERCISE

1. Stand or sit upright with an open posture.
2. Breathe in from your abdomen and out through your nose for four counts
3. Hold the breath for four counts.
4. Then breathe out of your mouth for four counts.

Continue with this for a couple of minutes before you go up to speak in order to help settle you. You can even do this discreetly in your seat in the meeting room before it's your turn to get up and speak.

Power posing for increasing confidence

In the last chapter I mentioned Amy Cuddy's TED talk *Your Body Language Shapes Who You Are* in the context of bringing your personality into your talk. This talk also provides fascinating insight into controlling our nerves too. She talks about how cortisol (a stress hormone) can increase in our bodies when we are under pressure. However, through our mind body connection, we can actually control our levels of stress. Her research findings are that when we adopt a powerful pose for as little as two minutes, our cortisol levels come down and we feel more confident. So, what is a powerful pose? It's basically anything that looks like open body language – for instance, chest out, arms out wide. It can be standing tall with your hands on hips or arms up above your head as if you are celebrating a huge win – typical pose of a sportsperson after a victory.

I highly recommend that you watch this video and then try it out for yourself.

Rituals that can help settle your nerves

For many people, they have an object or item of clothing that brings them luck. For others they have a routine that they always go through every time they have an important event. It's a way to get some semblance of control in an otherwise stressful situation.

Tennis player Rafael Nadal has many rituals – a lot of which we see when he is on court playing a match. When he comes out onto a tennis court to play a match he has two drink bottles that he lines up in front of his chair in a particular way. He does this with care and makes sure they always face the same way. If for some reason they get knocked over, he very carefully places them back in the exact position he intended. When he gets ready to serve, he goes through a sequence of gestures touching his face and adjusting his clothing. He does this every time he is about to throw the ball up in the air for a serve – sometimes taking longer than a player is allowed and risking a time penalty from the umpire. When Nadal won the French Open Men's Singles for a record tenth time, he stayed in the same hotel and suite as he had the very first time he won – has done that every year he competes in Paris. Whether all of this is superstition or just an elaborate ritual, it is something personal to him and part of his pre-match preparation.

What routines would help you get into the right frame of mind? Experiment with some of the suggestions in this chapter and find ones that can be part of your pre-match preparation. I mentioned power posing above – it's something that many of my clients have found extremely useful before going into an important meeting. They can easily find a way to go to a private space or the bathroom and just hold a powerful stance for two minutes without anyone else seeing them.

My simple ritual or process before a big speech is to get to the venue early and walk around the empty seminar room to get a feel for what it's like to stand at the front of the room. I then check that the slide deck and clicker are all working. When the delegates arrive, I go and mingle with them so that I have already made a connection with a few people and have some friendly faces to look at in the audience when it's my turn to speak. Then I focus on my breathing – reminding myself to keep breathing from my abdomen!

Getting in the zone with music

A few years ago I coached a newly appointed partner in an international law firm. She had been invited to speak at an industry conference at which she would be the only female speaker as well as the first time she had spoken on stage to a fairly large audience. Visualization didn't really work that well for her so we explored other resources. I wanted her to be able to find a way to get into a resourceful state – a shortcut to help her get in the 'zone' of feeling confident and excited about giving this presentation.

We found that listening to upbeat music helped her to get into this positive state. For her the song was Dolly Parton's '9 to 5'. You can't really get more upbeat than that! That is what she decided to listen to every time she rehearsed her presentation, on head phones in the taxi on the way to the conference and then at the back of the auditorium a few minutes before she was due to go on stage. This practice helped her get into a happy and confident frame of mind that also helped to distract her from anxieties about going into unknown territory and looking at hundreds of faces in the audience. It worked. From that day on, she now had a new benchmark – she had already successfully made it through a big presentation so the next time would be easier.

Music acts like a trigger. For many of us, when we hear a particular song it takes us back to a memory or association. For my client, she linked the feelings that song brought up to feeling confident about the presentation. Every time she heard the song it triggered positive feelings which helped reduce nervousness.

In the same way that visualization has been a powerful tool for athletes, listening to music is just as useful. I remember seeing this quite a lot in both the 2012 and 2016 Olympics – particularly with the swim events. Many of the competitors walked out from the locker room with headphones over their ears. We don't know what they were listening to – it may not even be music, it could be something else but either way it served to block out the noise outside to help the athlete get into the zone. It's part of their pre-match ritual.

I've given you a number of suggestions on how to mentally prepare to set yourself up for success. Of course, just like sitting on the couch imagining doing abdominal exercises to get a six pack won't work without putting in some physical effort, you can't deliver a confident presentation without proper preparation. The practical and mental preparation together will strengthen your foundation and help with controlling your nerves.

It's all about building your resilience to challenging and stressful situations. Resilience is not finite – you can increase it with any of the techniques above, helping you to adapt and become more comfortable in high pressure situations such as presentations and interviews.

TOP TIPS

- For the next week pay conscious attention to your thoughts and notice if you say anything less than positive. If you do find a way to say it differently.

- Watch Amy Cuddy's TED talk and then find a power pose that works for you. Practice it for 2 minutes every day for a week and notice if you feel more confident.

- Try out a guided meditation App and see if you like it.

- Commit to setting aside adequate time to prepare your content and rehearse your delivery as that will give your confidence a significant boost.

13

BODY LANGUAGE

In previous chapters we've looked at how to structure your material and make your content as interesting as possible. In this chapter we'll concentrate on aspects of non-verbal communication to help you better connect with your audience and enhance engagement. After all if the delivery isn't right then even the most stunning slides and entertaining stories can fall flat if the speaker is not on the same wavelength as the audience.

The key components of communication

Any time you are in a room with another person you are communicating – whether you say something or not. Much of our communication is non-verbal. The key areas of communication are:

- Verbal – the words we say
- Vocal – the tone of our voice, *how* we say it
- Visual – our body language or non-verbal communication

All three components are important, but *how* you say something with your tone and body language is much more persuasive than the actual words themselves.

In the early 1970s, Professor Mehrabian (University of California – Los Angeles) conducted a research study looking at all three components of communication mentioned above, dealing in particular with feelings and attitudes. The research focused on the meaning we attach to these components particularly when there is a mismatch – in that situation we are more likely to persuaded by tone, facial expressions and mannerisms.

A simple example of this is when someone is upset. You've probably been in a situation where you have noticed someone looking upset. When you ask if everything is all right they tend to say 'I'm OK'. However, their tone of voice and facial expressions say otherwise – they may be angry or tearful and that is quite visible in their face. They may even be holding tension in their body that is clear in their posture. All these clues lead to the conclusion that this person is anything but OK. This is because verbal and non-verbal communication is not congruent.

Simply put, all aspects of our communication channels need to be saying the same thing. That is why understanding how we communicate holistically is crucial to coming across as a persuasive and confident speaker. This is even more important when you have not met your audience before for example when you walk into the room at an interview or assessment centre, the panel will make instant judgments about you based upon your non-verbal communication before you have even said hello.

Your body language influences others

In the chapter covering confidence, I mentioned the research carried out by Amy Cuddy and her TED talk *Your Body Language May Shape Who You Are*. One of the key takeaways from that talk was the benefit of 'power posing' for two minutes to increase confidence before you go into a stressful situation like an interview or delivering a presentation. The other interesting fact was that as part of the research study two groups faced an interview panel. One group carried out the power pose before facing the panel and the other did not. The interview panel were not told about the power posing, but when asked which candidates they would offer a job to, they picked the ones who used power posing as part of their preparation. What's worth noting about this is that subtle changes in body language make an impact on your audience, even as far as persuading them to buy into what you are selling – whether that is a product, service or you as the most capable candidate. How you carry yourself says something about you.

My personal view is that your body language has to reflect your personality and be comfortable for you. Some presentation workshops or experts will teach you that you need to stand in a certain way or use your hands in a particular way to look 'professional'. I disagree with that. Of course you need to look professional but there is no need to be restrictive about your body language as long as it's not too distracting for the audience.

I once worked with a junior partner in a law firm helping her to prepare for a client seminar. As I sat through the dress rehearsal I noticed that she was standing on one leg – this continued for the entire length of her twenty minute slot! Just before I gave my feedback I asked if standing on one leg felt uncomfortable to which she replied 'no' because she didn't realize that's what she'd been doing! If the lectern behind which she had been standing had a privacy screen no one in the audience would have been any wiser but since we could see the open space below the table top it was clearly going to be a distraction for the audience. When something like that happens it draws the audience attention away from the message which you will have worked so hard to craft. On that occasion once we had identified the unconscious habit, she was able to focus on correcting her posture every time she rehearsed so that her delivery at the seminar went smoothly.

Facial expressions can be very powerful

Have you ever noticed how newscasters use facial expressions when they read the news on TV? Their job is to report the news in a factual way sitting behind a desk with very limited scope for movement or gestures. However, they still introduce changes in tone to reflect serious or light hearted news content. One of the ways they do this is through tone of voice, but they also use their facial muscles in a subtle way. If you turned off the volume on your TV set, you would still be able to tell if they were sharing a serious or light hearted piece of news by the look in their eyes, a smile or relaxed facial muscles.

More often than not, business speakers look far too serious when they speak – they have a stern look on their face which is not very welcoming for the audience. At the very least you want to look as relaxed as possible. Not all of your content will warrant a big smile of course, but subtle relaxing of the facial muscles makes a big difference. One of the easiest ways to make a connection with people you've never met before is to smile – remember this when you are in front of an interview panel – it will help you relax and breaks the ice with the audience. I've highlighted some examples of speakers for you to look at below. They all use their expressions to add emphasis to points they are making or add colour to their storytelling. The only way you will know how you come across when in front of an audience is to gather feedback. You can do this by asking someone in your audience or by recording yourself on video which, I think is the best way to get a true reflection of what is going on.

What to do with your hands

Hand gestures are a great way to enhance a point you want to make but until you know what feels right for you, it can feel awkward knowing what to do with your hands. In the next chapter we'll look at nervous habits such as playing with a pen, jangling coins in trouser pockets or playing with hair. These are tell tale signs that a speaker feels uncomfortable. As you become aware of these distracting movements, you can reduce them and replace them with more purposeful movement.

A starting point could be practising keeping your hands by your sides. This will take conscious effort but after a while it will feel less awkward. I used to clasp my hands in front of me quite a lot when I first started giving presentations. It wasn't too distracting but felt a bit restrictive and I was aware that it might communicate my lack of confidence. I had to 'unlearn' that unconscious habit and find something that looked a bit more neutral. Here's what worked for me:

Imagine holding a bag of heavy shopping in each hand by your sides – hold that pose for one minute and do it every time you rehearse for a presentation. If you can get comfortable with this neutral pose, then you can introduce hand gestures with purpose later to add emphasis to your words.

The other neutral pose for hands is lightly clasping fingers in front of you – you see politicians do this. This is a good compromise if you tend to fidget a lot.

Standing still versus moving around

Working on the basic principle that your movements should reflect your natural style as long as there is nothing too distracting for the audience, moving across the 'stage' can be effective in bringing energy and enthusiasm to your talk.

You don't have to move across the room at all if you don't want to or if the room is not set up to allow you to do so. If you take a look at Ken Robinson's TED talk mentioned in earlier chapters, you'll notice that he stands in one spot throughout his talk. This in no way detracts from his connection with the audience in a fairly large venue. His stationary stance gives him gravitas. The enthusiasm, energy and humour all come through the way in which he uses his tone of voice, facial expressions and hands.

Moving around and pacing can work for some people – Steve Jobs used to do it all the time when he was presenting at a product launch in large auditoriums. In earlier chapters we looked at the 2016 Public Speaking World Champion Darren Tay's speech. He was presenting to two thousand people in a large auditorium and had a big stage to navigate. For most of his speech he stood still but when he did move he did so with purpose. In order to connect with all parts of the room he moved from one side of the stage to the other at certain points of the speech. This wasn't random pacing, it was deliberate and timed to fit in with appropriate points he made.

There is no right or wrong way to think about movement across the front of the room. The real test is whether everyone can see you – you may need to incorporate movement to address both halves of the room like Darren Tay or you may be able to create the same effect by just slightly turning your body from side to side and making sure you make eye contact with every part of the audience.

Linking back to the concept of total communication of words, voice and body language, if there is a lectern or podium, try to get out from behind it – people trust you more when they can see you. Open body language gives the impression of confidence – similar to the practice of power posing using open stances that help you feel confident.

I'd recommend viewing examples of different speaker styles demonstrated by the following TED talks. Each speaker has their own unique style. They all move differently and use hand gestures differently. What they all have in common is that they are connecting with their audience and look as if they are moving naturally. Take a look and then have a think about how you use your body when you speak.

Tony Robbins – *Why We Do What We Do*

To give you some background, Tony is an American peak performance coach who runs multi day seminars which means he is on stage for a lengthy amount of time and sometimes each day can be over 10 hours long. His audience is typically large – ranging from two to ten thousand. I've been in many of them over the years! For someone like this to speak for just a short amount of time is a challenge – if you watch the video you'll see that he acknowledges this up front in his talk. For the purposes of this chapter though, I'd like to focus on his use of body language – it's very expressive, but not overly so. As a word of warning, there are some swear words – used deliberately for shock effect.

He's a big guy who has a big personality which is authentic for him. I've seen many people in a similar industry space try to copy his style and it doesn't work for them as well. Each speaker has their own unique way of speaking and moving and that's what they should work with, not try to copy someone else. What is useful about studying other speakers is to see how they work the room and connect with the audience.

Tony walks around the stage quit a bit – almost pacing too much, but then he balances this with stopping purposefully to make a point and look the audience in the eye. Watch how he uses hand gestures and facial expressions to emphasize points. He even clicks his fingers. This is someone who owns the stage, uses his whole body to bring lots of energy and enthusiasm – perhaps a bit shouty at times which is not to everyone's liking but this is tempered with vocal variety. A loud shouty delivery throughout an entire presentation would not work and turns the audience off – I have seen it happen quite often though. We'll focus more on voice in a later chapter.

Julian Treasure – *How to Speak so that People Want to Listen*

In contrast to Tony Robins, Julian Treasure doesn't move across the stage much but that doesn't mean his impact upon the audience is any less. He uses hand gestures to emphasize points and describe concepts visually, but the rest of his body remains in the same position on stage for most of his talk. I'll be coming back to this talk later when we look at verbal communication as Julian demonstrates how to do this really well.

Susan Cain – *The Power of Introverts*

Susan uses her hands all the way through her talk. What's interesting to note is that she clasps her hands when she is not using them to 'talk with'. Some people might say that clasping hands is a sign of nervousness but I don't think that the way Susan uses her hands is awkward at all. If she'd clasped her hands like that throughout the talk without any variety then that might look awkward – this was something that I used to do before I worked at finding a way to feel comfortable with my hands at my side. I now use my hands to 'talk with' like Susan does.

Simon *Sinek – How Great Leaders Inspire Action*

Simon has a very small amount of space on the stage to work with compared to the other speakers mentioned above. He also has issues with a defective hand held microphone for the first few minutes of the talk until someone hands him another. None of this throws him off course. He maintains good eye contact and uses his free hand to create gestures. I chose this particular example because Simon uses a flip chart to draw on and add a visual element to his content. As he does this, he maintains a connection with the audience almost all the time by only turning his body slightly towards the flip chart and keeping a fairly open stance in order to maintain rapport with them. This is a good example of how to use a flip chart when presenting. The worst thing you can do is to turn your back on your audience, especially to look at your slides. Find a way to do that from the corner of your eye by way of a quick glance or just turning your torso slightly.

I wanted to discuss these four very different styles to bring home the point about uniqueness. No speaker is the same and yet they use their body language to add energy and emphasis to their message. There are no rules about how you should stand or what to do with your hands – the various ways in which these four speakers do this proves that. The key is to balance what fits you and ensure that whatever you are doing does not distract the audience.

Getting comfortable with and understanding the impact of your body language can take a bit of time and you may need to practise elsewhere if you don't get to speak or present that often.

EXERCISE

Stand up right with your shoulders aligned and your feet pointing forwards, hip distance apart, with your weight evenly distributed. Imagine a piece of string pulling you up from the top of your head and roots or steel rods coming out of the bottom of your feet and running into the ground, anchoring you. This is a powerful stance and should help you feel centred. Practice getting used to what this feels like.

You can practise this pose when you are standing on a train, waiting in line or even for a couple of minutes when you brush your teeth!

Maintaining appropriate eye contact

Making eye contact when addressing an audience is important – it's a key part of connecting and maintaining rapport with your audience. It seems obvious that you would want to look at your audience when you speak to them but not everyone finds this easy to do at first. Think about what it feels like when someone is talking to you but doesn't make eye contact. It's uncomfortable isn't it? It may not be intentional and can be due to a lack of confidence, but when someone doesn't make eye contact we can feel as if they are being evasive and we are less persuaded by what they have to say.

That is why ensuring that you look at your audience is essential. There is a fine balance between making sure you do look at people for a few seconds and then going too far and staring at them for too long as that is also uncomfortable. If at first you are not too keen at looking at people directly in the eye, start by looking in the general direction of their heads without necessarily locking eyes. Every time you present, challenge yourself to make eye contact with two more people each time until it becomes natural and you no longer need to consciously think about it.

Why energy is important

Your energy, vitality and enthusiasm are what will bring your presentation to life. That will look different for all of us – we show enthusiasm to differing degrees and in different ways. However you choose to reflect this in your natural style, one key thing to remember is this: you need to seem interested in your topic and demonstrate an interest for it, because if you don't then why should the audience? They will take their lead from you.

It can of course be the other way round – you might come in all loud and bouncy and the audience is flat and hard to read. In that situation, tone it down a bit and meet them closer to where they are at first and as they warm to you, gradually increase your level of energy.

Your enthusiasm can come through your tone of voice, your hand gestures or even something as simple as a smile.

The main takeaway in this chapter is that the power of your communication lies in more than just the words you speak.

TOP TIPS

- When you rehearse your talk, make sure your words and non-verbal communication are saying the same thing – they have to be congruent.

- Watch as many other speakers as you can – whether in person at seminars or in your office, and online on platforms such as TED and Toastmasters. See how they use gestures and movements to get a feel for how you might like to hone your style.

- Record yourself practising on video – this will help you identify whether you need to rein in any distracting movements or make them bigger so that they help you add emphasis to a point you make.

14

GETTING RID OF BAD HABITS

The main focus of this book is to help you create the best presentation possible and be able to deliver in a way that both engages the audience and showcases your personality. In order to achieve that I've repeatedly recommended rehearsal and feedback as ways to set you up for success by ironing out any kinks that could reduce the impact of your presentation. Those kinks might include bad habits.

What are bad habits?

I would say 'bad habits' are those that distract your audience or get in the way of you being your absolute best when presenting.

In earlier chapters we looked at bad habits in the context of slide design and the importance of putting in the appropriate amount of effort to ensure that they enhance the audience experience. A bad habit in relation to slides is throwing all your points into the slide deck and listing them as endless bullet points.

In this chapter, we'll look at other non 'techie' areas where bad habits can creep in and how to make improvements.

Apologizing to get sympathy

Don't ever do this. Why do people generally apologize during their presentations? There are a number of scenarios.

Starting off with an apology creates a negative focus for your presentation. Believe it or not, I've heard speakers apologize for their delivery being flat as they have had a late night or lack of sleep for whatever reason. The audience does not care and this actually makes you look unprofessional. Even if you are feeling under par, focus on the audience experience and think about your energy and body language needing to be as high as possible for the short amount of time you are up on your feet speaking.

The topic may be a little dry or technical but necessary for the audience to know about. Setting the scene by apologizing for the content being 'boring' serves no one and doesn't get the speaker off the hook for a boring presentation, contrary to what they may think. The better way to approach an uninspiring topic is put some effort in and weave in interesting analogies, stories or visuals. Failing that, just resist drawing attention to the fact that they may be bored – this is a sure fire way to help them get there!

Perhaps the most common reason for an apology is when presenters run out of time and rush through the latter stages of the talk by clicking rapidly through the slides and drawing attention to the fact that the talk will have to be wrapped up soon so not all remaining points can be explored fully. This is really bad. It leaves the audience with the impression that the speaker has not had the courtesy to prepare properly and they feel cheated out of parts that now have to be skipped. This is why it is so important to prepare your content to fit the time slot allowed and to rehearse adequately so that you don't put yourself in this difficult situation in the first place.

If you are delivering your presentation at an interview this will be a great opportunity to showcase your personality, knowledge and skills. Part of the skillset prospective employers might be looking for include the ability to plan well, time keeping and 'a can do' attitude. If for whatever reason you are underprepared on the day, I would recommend you focus on what you have got going for you and do the best you can in the moment without drawing unnecessary attention by apologizing. Of course the best way to tackle this is to prepare well but sometimes other priorities get in the way and things don't go to plan.

Using slides as a crutch

I mention this point quite often throughout the book. The slides, should you choose to use them, are your support act. You are the presentation. If you have created the slides for maximum audience experience then they will be more image based than text based. However some speakers add in plenty of text onto each slide so that they remember what to say – using the slides as a teleprompter. This is very bad practice for two reasons. The slides become too crowded for the audience to follow plus if you are reading them as well, then inevitably you will break rapport and end up turning your back on the audience.

If you must have some sort of prompt, use notecards or a mind map to put on the table or laptop nearby. Go back to the section on using notes to check best practice for this.

Another reason not to rely on slides for jogging your memory is that sometimes the technology lets you down unexpectedly – your slides may not work at all or may be out of alignment. Be ready to speak without slides.

Asking for more time during your presentation

Lack of preparation and rehearsal often leads to presenters misjudging their time slot. A really bad habit is to ask the chairperson or event host for more time during your presentation. By doing this you put them in a difficult spot as they have to manage the timings for the entire agenda, plus you clearly showcase that you are under prepared.

Your time slot may also be reduced through no fault of your own, for example if other speakers go on too long.

If for any reason you have to cut short your presentation, resist apologizing and mentally make the adjustment you need to cut content but ensuring you make an impact by still finishing with your planned ending. If you have to miss out slides you no longer have time for then pause for a moment, minimize your slide deck and skip to the one you want to jump to then restart your slideshow. Disguise the fact that you are missing slides out by stating that you are looking for a particular slide you want to focus on.

Fidgeting while speaking

Fidgeting while speaking is mostly unconscious – we do it without realizing, usually when we feel nervous. This can show up in lots of ways, for example:

- playing with long hair
- touching the face repeatedly
- playing with a ring
- clicking a spring loaded pen or the pen lid on and off
- jangling keys or coins in trouser pockets

This type of thing is distracting for the audience, especially if the fidgeting makes a noise! Becoming aware as to whether you are a fidget is the first step. The next step is to find a way to stop doing it – the easiest way is to swap it with another habit. If you are used to picking something up in your hands when speaking because it feels uncomfortable not to hold something, then find a pen that doesn't click or hold small notecards with your key points written on them. This will help you transition from fidgeting to holding something with purpose to gradually feeling comfortable not holding anything at all. The more focus you bring to creating a new habit of what to do with your hands the quicker you can let go of the unconscious movements.

Pacing, swaying or shifting from side to side when standing to speak

Nervous energy can lead to other unintentional movements such pacing up and down the front of the room. Moving from side to side is not bad in itself, but when it is constant then it detracts from the audience experience. There are plenty of speakers who, as part of their natural delivery style, move from one side of the stage to the other. The key is to keep it all in proportion and stop from time to time, otherwise you are making the audience move their heads from side to side as if watching a tennis match! When you move, do so with purpose rather than randomly pacing. One way to improve upon this is to decide that you will stand still for key points in your presentation – such as when you move from one point to another. Write this down in your notes if you are using any – highlight the points where you want to stand still to make the point.

Similarly, another unconscious habit is not standing still with an aligned posture. For example leaning on one leg more than the other or swaying on the spot. These kind of poses tend to give off the impression of unprofessionalism or being too relaxed. This is not always a problem – it depends on where you are and what type of meeting you are in, but if it's a client presentation or interview panel then it matters.

Again, the starting point is becoming aware that you may have a tendency to do these things – get someone to watch you while you rehearse and interrupt you so that you can keep correcting your posture to one that is balanced with your weight equally distributed between both feet.

'Winging it' or hoping for the best

Perhaps the most annoying habit in my view, is the one where speakers don't invest enough time in preparing or leave it to the last minute and think that they can wing it on the day. In Chapter 4 I covered the value of rehearsal. Without rehearsal, there is no way to know how long your speech will be or how your material sounds out loud. Preparing a speech or presentation to a high standard takes proper planning. If you are interviewing for a new role then arguably the stakes are higher as you want to stand out from the crowd – definitely a strong argument for planning rather than winging it!

Speaking too fast

I recently ran a two-day workshop on presentation skills during which time the delegates have the opportunity to work on a speech and deliver it several times after getting feedback from the rest of the group. At least two members of the group received feedback that they were speaking too fast and could benefit from slowing down the pace of their delivery. To which, both replied that they had acknowledged during their speeches that they were probably going too fast but did it anyway because they could finish quicker and get it over with! Clearly there were some issues around nervousness which we worked on, but speaking fast to 'get it over with' is quite a common occurrence.

A fast pace can occur unconsciously as well. When there is an adrenalin rush, our breathing quickens and in turn we tend to speak faster.

With time and practice this can be improved. You want to aim for a natural conversational pace. By natural I mean natural for you. Some people speak quite fast anyway – if this is you, make sure you introduce pause breaks in between sections for the benefit of the audience.

Speaking too quietly

If your audience can't hear you then all your hard work in preparing for your presentation will be undone. Some people are naturally quietly spoken for others nerves can have an effect on volume. This is where practice really pays off. When you rehearse in front of others or record yourself practising you will be able to gauge how to match the volume to the size of the room. Sometimes you only get one chance to make an impression and you want to make sure you are heard when you get that chance. Focus on the person in the back row and project your voice to them – visualize it happening and breathe from your abdomen to ensure you have enough air to give you some power. Keep your focus on the audience experience to help you remember to adjust your volume – it can be quite easy to fall into the trap of focusing inwards and worrying about just getting to the end in high pressure situations such as interview presentations. Go back over Chapter 16 for more details on voice control.

Reducing filler words

Filler words are single words or short sentences such as:

- *um*
- *er*
- *ah*
- *so*
- *like*
- *right*
- *you know*

We use these in our everyday conversations and there is nothing wrong with them, except when they appear too often during a presentation – they can be a distraction. Too many of these filler words can detract from an otherwise high-quality presentation if the audience perceives them to be distracting. When we are nervous or thinking of what to say next, we naturally want to fill the silence and so these words creep in.

A suggestion for reducing these types of words in your presentation is to swap them for pauses. Whenever you are thinking of what to say next, mentally stop yourself from saying anything, take a breath and pause for a couple of seconds. It may seem like an eternity to you but for the audience it's hardly any time at all, plus it gives them time to process what you just shared.

This is something that you improve over time.

Negative self talk and reframing it

When we looked at overcoming nerves in Chapter 12, we discussed the negative chatter that runs through our minds for example, when worrying about forgetting the speech or a shaky voice. We get what we focus on. Constantly focusing on what could go wrong is a bad habit. Go back and look at the recommendations for reframing unhelpful self talk if this is a problem for you.

Remember to switch off your mobile phone

This seems really obvious, right? I'm sure you've been in a seminar or meeting and someone's phone starts ringing – usually with some amusing ringtone that generates some chuckles from the audience. For the speaker this is very annoying as it

---

EXERCISE

1. Practice a speech in front of a friend or colleague and get them to jot down the number of times you use any of the above filler words. That is the first step – the awareness of how often you use filler words.

2. Run through the same presentation again but this time ask your friend to interrupt you by shouting out or using a bell or similar. This will be annoying for you as you will be constantly interrupted but what's happening is that your unconscious habit is being broken so that you can start to create a new one – replacing the unnecessary words with pauses.

interrupts the flow of their presentation and quite frankly it's disrespectful to them and the rest of the audience. The last thing you want is for your phone to go off during your interview or assessment. Of course people forget to turn off their phones from time to time and inevitably the one time they don't want the phone to ring it does. The way I make this work for me is to keep my phone on silent when at work and then when I get home I take it off silent mode. That way I don't get caught out. I'm also used to checking my phone again before I go into a meeting or even the cinema to make sure. Keeping your phone on silent might not be practical for you. Maybe you could keep a checklist or set a reminder on your phone so that you double-check the ringer is actually off before an important meeting.

Forgetting to eat or drink

Strictly speaking this might not be classed as a bad habit but perhaps it leans more towards taking better care of yourself. You may forget or just not feel up to eating something before a presentation or assessment due to nerves, however at the very least your tummy might make rumbling sounds, which is not very professional! The other thing to bear in mind is that lack of nutrition can affect your concentration and energy levels which sometimes causes light-headedness. Similarly not drinking enough water can leave you feeling less than your best. Plan ahead and have something small like a protein or muesli bar to tide you over as well as keeping a bottle of water handy.

TOP TIPS

- Always have a plan B – if you are running short of time for whatever reason, know where to cut your content short without unnecessarily drawing attention to it.

- Practice drills with a friend or colleague to break the habit of filler words or fidgeting moves by asking them to interrupt you whenever you use them.

- Don't make excuses for lack of preparation – your audience won't be interested – just jump into giving them value.

- Get into the habit of checking your phone is on silent before any meeting – this will save you from embarrassment.

- Always keep water and snacks to hand in order to maintain focus and energy levels.

15

VERBAL COMMUNICATION

Your voice reflects who you are – your personality. We also communicate our emotions through our voices. Your voice is unique – it is such a distinct sound that people recognize us even when they can't see us for example when we speak on the telephone. Think about family members or famous voices you hear as voice-overs on TV adverts – there are some very unmistakable voices.

When you speak, then, whether you are in an interview, team meeting or pitching situation in front of an audience that doesn't know you, your voice will give them a certain impression about you. You could be the best person for the job but if you are quietly spoken with a monotone style, then others may think you are timid, not very assertive and lacking in confidence and competence. Alternatively, your normal speaking style may be louder and more direct which some may interpret as arrogant. There is no right or wrong way to sound – what's important is to have an awareness that we can control how we want to sound. The aim is to find a way to help people perceive you the way you would like them to perceive you.

What I'd like to explore in this chapter is how to match your voice to your intended message. That doesn't mean drastically changing how you sound to adopt a different persona or character, but making adjustments in order to make your communication impactful.

How do you sound?

You probably don't think about your voice much, it's just something that is there. We tend to take our voice for granted until we feel unwell and maybe lose it for a while – or until we hear it from a new perspective. When I first got started in my legal career I used to be able to dictate letters that would later be typed up a secretary in the team. The thing about dictating into a machine is that you have to keep rewinding to listen back and make sure you are happy with what's recorded before you send it out for typing. Over the years I had to do this hundreds of times and it made me cringe to hear my own voice back – it took me a long time to get used to hearing a voice that sounded different to the one in my head! Most of us don't like the way we sound when we hear it played back to us.

EXERCISE

Read out a page from a magazine or book and record it. What others hear is not what you hear – how does your voice match up to what you thought you sounded like?

There are many variables to our speech patterns – speed, tonality and volume, as well as how your body affects your voice. With practice, you can choose how to adjust these to better connect with your target audience.

Your voice box is a very powerful instrument

Knowing your material and being able to share your knowledge is only one part of the presentation process. We spend much more time worrying about *what* we want to say and not nearly enough time thinking about *how* we want to say it. In Chapter 13, I talked about Professor Mehrabian's research on the meaning attached to communication and how, when there is a mismatch, we are more persuaded by tonality and physiology than the actual words that are said. *How* you share your content is the bigger part.

Sound comes out of our mouth when the vocal chords vibrate as air is pushed through them via the lungs – this action affects the pitch, tone and volume. By adjusting our pace and tone, we can introduce variety which keeps our audience engaged. The way we breathe is therefore very important in being able to control our vocal variety.

When I first started working on improving my presentations, one of the things I struggled with was my naturally soft voice. To help me find a way to get more volume, I decided to take singing lessons. My singing teacher had me doing deep breathing exercises using the abdomen as opposed to shallower chest breathing. Of course, breathing is something we all do unconsciously – but not all of us have the right technique, especially for presentation situations. The exercises made me focus on proper technique, and really opened my eyes to the necessity for breathing the right way. This made a big difference – not just to my volume – as it allowed me to control my voice better and helped me cope with nerves. When the adrenalin kicks in we tend to switch to shallow breathing and that is not helpful! The exercises made me focus on proper technique.

Diaphragmatic breathing is a staple for singers – being able to control your breath via smooth passage out rather than being restricted by any tension in your chest. Think of shallow chest breathing as being like having one foot on the gas and the other on the brake. I don't want to get too technical here, I just want to highlight that ideally you want strength and stamina and breath that you control, so that when you are at the front of the room speaking, you can make sure you have enough breath to carry on with the whole sentence.

EXERCISE

Stand in front of a mirror so that you can see your entire torso. Ensure good open posture by holding your head straight with your chin level to the ground. Let go of any tension in your shoulders, pull them back making sure they are not slumped or rounded. This will open up your ribcage to allow your lungs to expand. Have your feet hip distance apart – imagining a piece of string pulling through your body from feet to head.

Then take a deep breath, breathing in through your nose then and exhaling through your mouth. What do you notice happening? Which parts of your body moved?

If you are doing this the right way, then you will see your tummy expand outwards and your chest and shoulders will remain still. If you noticed that your shoulders moved upwards and your chest expanded out, then have another go.

This time, put your hand on your stomach. Think of your stomach as an expanding balloon as you take in a breath, without moving your ribcage or shoulders.

Focus mentally and inhale.

When you exhale, relax your stomach muscles and easily let the air out. Not much effort is required – there is no need to push the air out. Be aware of any tension in the muscles. Again focus on your breath and relaxing your muscles as you let the air out.

Create a habit of stopping twice a day to do this.

The right pace or speed

Every one of us speaks at a different pace, one that fits with our natural style. Some of us speak fast and others speak a lot slower. Speaking too slowly might come across as less knowledgeable or uncertain, and in previous chapters, we've covered how nerves can accelerate the pace of your speech.

This is where breathing from the diaphragm really helps you to control unwanted increased pace. Altering your pace deliberately, however, can be very effective when you want to add emphasis to points in your speech. For example, slowing down when you are making an important point signposts it for the audience, and you can inject enthusiasm and energy by speeding parts of your delivery up. For an example of someone who speaks fast to inject energy into his speech, watch Shawn Achor's TED talk *The Happy Secret to Better Work*.

Varying tone or pitch – avoiding monotone

In Chapter 13, I mentioned newscasters and how you can tell from their facial expressions whether the news piece is serious or light hearted. They also do this with their voices, adding emphasis and impact to certain words by varying their pitch and tone.

A pitch is a particular frequency of sound that you hear – it is the height or depth of the range of your voice. Think about all the individual notes on a piano keyboard. At one end you have a high pitch and at the opposite end you have a low pitch. A mix of frequencies in sound is described as timbre. Timbre (sometimes described as tone) represents the quality or fullness of the sound. This is affected by many things, including our physiology and breath.

It is alleged that Margaret Thatcher had voice coaching to adjust the tone of her voice in order to make it sound lower and deeper. Whether or not there is any truth about her receiving any coaching, it is clear from watching video footage on YouTube that her voice did change. Early on in her political career her voice sounded much higher in comparison to footage from the early 1980s, during her second term as Prime Minister, when we can hear that the sound is much deeper. Her deeper voice here lends her more gravitas than the higher-pitched – almost shrill – tone that we hear in earlier footage. We are persuaded by lower voices because we tend to associate depth with power.

You want to use a tone that makes your audience think of you as competent or even an expert.

However, just picking one tone (not too high, and not uncomfortably low) is not quite enough. Monotone is speaking at one pitch or note – like hitting the same key on a piano keyboard constantly, and after a while it becomes incredibly boring and possibly even quite annoying. Lack of vocal variety is one of the main reasons why listeners switch off. People have very short attention spans so this can be a problem, but by using your vocal range to communicate your emotions, you have the ability to make your audience feel a certain way – inspired, motivated, sympathetic or confident in what you have to offer. Start paying attention to people around you – what do they sound like? We can learn a lot from observing and listening to others.

EXERCISE

Watch the news on TV – then jot down the changes in the newscaster's pitch and tone. What type of stories are linked to high pitch sounds and conversely what about lower pitch? Serious news items are usually delivered at a lower pitch. Similarly with tonality – notice the shift from neutral, emotionless almost monotone to warmer colourful tones when moving from serious topics to light hearted news items. This is also a great exercise to go through the next time you are sitting in a meeting or presentation. Listen out for how other people match their vocal range to points they are making. This will help you focus on your own delivery style when you have to give your next presentation.

A few years ago I had organized a client seminar, inviting over 100 key client contacts to an evening seminar covering industry updates followed by networking. I had arranged for two external speakers to come and talk about their specialist area – the theme was industrial diseases. They could not have been more different. The first speaker was very conversational and engaging. He had very simple slides showing photographs and told stories through patient case studies. Everyone in the audience could follow along with what he had shared and actually enjoyed his talk because he entertained us. One of the ways in which he did that was to use vocal variety when he shared his stories – he even gave voices to his patients. The second speaker had too many slides that all looked very similar and didn't use any case studies or stories. His content was all very factual and difficult to digest. What made this particular occasion memorable for me was that halfway through his presentation I looked around the audience. A few seats along to the left of me someone had fallen asleep and the glasses perched on the nose were at the point of slipping off. To the right of me a few rows in front, another person had fallen asleep and they were actually drooling. The problem was that in addition to having boring content, this speaker had a boring voice. He spoke in one gear only and never mixed it up which resulted in some members of the audience literally falling asleep. I thought it a wasted opportunity – this particular expert had a very good reputation for providing written reports but clearly in person his delivery didn't match up.

Until you hear yourself as you present, you will never really know how others might perceive you, which is why I strongly recommend recording your voice when you rehearse so that you can make adjustments if needed. You don't need to adopt a theatrical range of voices, just be aware that some vocal variety is necessary to keep your audience engaged. If you are clever about it, you can deliberately add emphasis or signpost parts of talk by changing up your vocal delivery in parts.

> **EXERCISE**
>
> Read out a passage in a fiction book and use pitch variation. Play around with different voices and record it so that you can listen to it and get a feel for what you could do differently in your next presentation, especially when you are relaying client case studies or sharing a story.

Playing with volume

I mentioned earlier that I had a challenge with not being able to speak loud enough in front of a larger audience. You need your audience to be able to hear you. Adding volume can help you sound confident – if you speak too softly people may think what you have to say is not very important. Also, if they have to work too hard to listen to you they will probably just switch off and stop trying. However, deliberately dropping to a whisper or raising your voice at times can be very effective. As human beings when someone whispers we naturally want lean in to catch what is being said, in case it's a secret! By cleverly dropping your volume to a soft whisper you can draw your audience in. Of course this isn't something you can use in all speeches but a good place to incorporate it might be when you tell a story. For an example of how to do this, see the Julian Treasure video suggestion at the end of this chapter.

Speaking on the telephone

The main focus of this book is about delivering presentations in front of a live audience. I personally think that any time you are communicating with others you are presenting in some form or other. Speaking on the telephone is another way of presenting. We communicate through emails a lot these days but much of communication is over the phone as well. What's interesting about phone conversations is that we obviously can't see our audience and so there is much more emphasis on how we sound. All the ideas for vocal variety above are just as relevant, if not even more crucial to phone conversations. You can tell if someone sounds confident or hesitant can't you?

This was something I was very conscious of during the early part of my legal career. In the interests of saving costs, many of the court hearings I attended were telephone conference calls with the Judge and all relevant parties. The good thing was that no one could see how nervous I might have looked, but I had to be very careful of how I sounded because your voice can give you away! My plan of action was to have a list of talking points written out in advance so that I could easily refer to them if I was called upon by the Judge. The last thing

I needed was to get flustered while scrambling through my file of papers. In a way, my preparation and research for these type of telephone hearings was very similar to how I prepare for my presentations today.

Whether you are speaking to internal colleagues, clients or suppliers, you want to come across as persuasive, knowledgeable, trustworthy and approachable. As mentioned earlier, a lot of communication happens via email but telephone is still relevant in the workplace. You may need to sell an idea or product or negotiate better terms for a contract such as booking a conference venue or dealing with suppliers. The way you come across matters because the person on the other end of the line will be influenced by what you say and how you say it.

Finally... a great example to bring it all together

By now you'll be familiar with the references to many TED talks I have made in order to give you some additional resources to illustrate the tips and techniques I recommend. I'd like to suggest watching Julian Treasure's TED talk *How to Speak so that People Want to Listen*. This particular TED talk has been viewed over 20 million times and is listed as one of the top 20 TED talks of all time. In my personal opinion, Julian has a great voice – one that you could listen to for ages without getting bored. When you watch it, look at it from two perspectives. The first time, just watch it and listen to how he uses the full range of his voice. There is a deep resonance in his voice that conveys confidence. He plays with vocal variety – at times using a softer pitch then contrasting with a more forceful sound and more pace.

Now watch it again. Pay attention to how Julian demonstrates the different aspects of our voices such as volume and pace, mentioned throughout this chapter, including vocal exercises you can do to warm up for a presentation.

I want to encourage you to think of your voice box as a very valuable part of your toolkit when it comes to presenting and communication in general. By adapting your voice you can add emphasis, signpost key messages and create interest for your audience.

TOP TIPS

- Always record yourself as you rehearse so that you can make any necessary adjustments to inject variety or emphasis in your delivery.
- Practice deep breathing whenever you can – perhaps if you are waiting in a queue. The more you get a feel for your diaphragm, the easier it will be to control your breath in pressured situations.

16

COPING WITH THE UNEXPECTED

Even with thorough preparation and rehearsal the unexpected could happen – things could go wrong on the day of your presentation. Even though many things may be out of your control, there are still precautions you can take to make sure you give yourself the best possible chance of success.

A word of caution – never try something new for the first time in your presentation such as including last minute content or changing the order of things on the spur of the moment. Stick to what you have prepared and rehearsed for, otherwise you are asking for trouble.

Let's take a look at what you can do to minimize any mishaps or deal with obstacles.

Check out your environment

I always like to see the room that I will be speaking in before an event if I haven't been there before. This gives me the chance to visualize the space and take account of any limitations in the room such as the location of the big screen or issues with lighting. Of course this isn't always possible but sometimes I can still get a look at the room by other means: for example, I might ask my host to take a photo and send it to me, or if it's a big event, hotels and conference venues often have photos or 360 degree views on their website. In the absence of any of these, I aim to get to the venue early, before the audience are due to arrive so I can stand at the front of the room and get a feel for the environment.

Early on in your career the most likely venue you may be speaking in is the boardroom or another meeting room in your office in which case there is every opportunity to check out the space in advance. If you are going for an interview or attending an assessment centre, however, then you won't have the chance to do this – even if you don't, though, you should still get there early on the day of your presentation. In fact, you should get there early even if you will have the chance to check out the venue, so that you can check the layout of the room, the running order, and IT or Audio Visual (AV) facilities, and find out who is responsible for the technical set up and make contact with them so that they can help you with linking up your slides etc.

Check out the location of the screen and computer keyboard. It's good to find out where the projector is so that you know how to avoid standing in the beam of light as it projects your slides onto the big screen.

Test the remote clicker if there is one – which buttons do you need to press to move your slides in the right direction? It seems like a simple thing but not all clickers are the same – the last thing you want is to be thrown off course when you bring up the wrong slide by mistake and get flustered in the middle of your presentation. As it is such a small item, I usually take my own remote clicker as a back-up – sometimes they don't even have one in the room as the set-up is a PC keyboard sitting on a lectern or podium. At least if you have a clicker you have the option of coming out from behind the lectern and getting closer to the audience or moving around the room.

If possible, go over to the laptop or PC and click through your first few slides to check if everything looks ok. If you have embedded any video or audio links, click those to check if they play as they should and that the sound levels are right. When it comes to sound, you need to make sure there are speakers in the room that work. The in-built speakers on a laptop are not loud enough to create a good enough sound experience to fill a room unless the audience is really small. A few years ago, I was due to give a presentation to a department of about 100 attendees in a big lecture theatre. I arrived early as I usually like to do in order to set up my laptop and check everything would work as planned. Normally in a venue like that, there is a central control panel that controls the speakers and mirrors the display from my laptop. For some reason, I couldn't get the speakers to work and neither could the AV person for the organization. In the end, I had to position my laptop near a microphone on the lectern, that is usually meant for the presenter, and play sound through that in a round about way. So even with designated technical support I couldn't proceed as planned. I now have my own mini speakers which I always carry with me – just in case!

I wouldn't advise this, but if you plan to play a video clip from the internet because you don't have a downloaded version, then make sure there is a strong enough internet connection in the room beforehand and definitely check this out for yourself when you arrive. Similarly, you may want to show other websites or content through the internet depending on your topic. Even in this day and age, there are plenty of dead zones and not all rooms in a building have strong wifi connections. Again, this may not be something you can control – at least be prepared to miss out the video if you can't play it. Throughout this book I've used TED talks to give you examples of speakers demonstrating different styles and techniques; I also use them in my workshops and presentations. Sometimes, even when I have checked in advance with the venue that they will have wifi connectivity, when I turn up I find that it's not very good – which means I can't play my video. In that situation, I will describe that concept and then give references for my audience to go away and watch it online later, or sometimes I use my mobile phone as a local hotspot to connect to the internet. The other recommendation I have for the smooth running of your presentation is to have a separate browser tab open for your video rather than embedding the link into your slides. That way if you can't play your video, your slides work without it. If you do have a good connection then when the time comes, just walk over to the keyboard and switch from slideshow to browser mode. Your audience won't mind.

If you are preparing for an interview or assessment centre presentation, then keep it really simple and leave out any multi media. That way you reduce the scope for things going wrong plus it's highly unlikely that your slide design skills are being tested in those circumstances anyway. What the prospective employer is looking for is your ability to get your message across and engage an audience confidently.

Checking your slides and hand outs are ready

Wherever possible, if you intend to show slides then use your own laptop. However this isn't always an option and you may have to send your slides over to someone else in advance for them to set everything up in the presentation room ready for you to just get up and speak when it's your turn.

I've worked with a number of government organizations where email attachments are blocked from email exchange due to firewall issues – in the interests of safeguarding against viruses. This is completely understandable; however, it does create a bit of a dilemma if you are trying to send over a file with your slides. Large attachments can also cause problems (for example, slides with lots of images, like I use), so it's happened to me a few times. Sometimes it is possible to upload your file to a cloud storage folder such as Dropbox or GoogleDrive. You could take your slides on a memory stick to upload on the day but there is a risk it may not load; or again, some organizations won't allow you to use your memory stick on their system, for cybersecurity reasons.

The best course of action is to ask in advance what the preferred method of file transfer is – never leave it to chance or assume it'll be ok because trust me, I have seen plenty of people get caught out. If you have been given a task to prepare a presentation in advance for an interview or assessment centre that requires you to use slides, ask the organizers if you're required to send the slides in advance or if you need to bring your own memory stick.

One last precaution for offsite presentations – email the slides to yourself. That way even if your memory stick doesn't work, there is a way to forward your email to someone on the day for uploading onto the system.

In Chapter 9, I recommended a few tips to ensure that your slides travel well. Let's recap: remember that other people may have a different version of PowerPoint than you which could affect the way your content is displayed, so group your images and text together on every slide so that they don't move out of place. Keep it simple with very few moving parts – that way there is less scope for things to go wrong!

If you are using printed hand outs either in addition to or instead of slides, make sure you have enough copies. If someone else is taking care of the printing, allow enough time to organize this. Again, I've seen things get lost in the system for various reasons and the hand outs don't arrive as planned. I take clean copies with me that can be photocopied on site at the last minute if needed.

In addition to your back-up slides, it's always a good idea to think about any other equipment you might need – such as power cables, batteries, pens for Flipchart paper and enough paper to write on if you are using a Flipchart as your visual aid.

Tech problems during your presentation

Even when you are set up and ready to go, everything looking good, sometimes tech issues arise during the presentation. It could be something simple like a cable being pulled out of a connection by someone arriving late or accidentally knocking the slides out of slideshow mode like the expert example I shared in an earlier chapter. If something goes wrong with your visuals – pause for a moment to decide what you want to do. Usually the issue is quite straightforward and can be identified in few seconds. You could acknowledge the hitch and ask the audience to bear with you while you check what's happened, or perhaps get the audience to discuss a question or idea with their neighbours for a few minutes while you try and fix the problem or get some help with it.

If all else fails and you can't get your slides to work, use a printed version of your slide deck as a prompt or your mind map from your preparation stage to carry on. Be ready to speak without slides. The important thing to remember here is to keep calm and look as if you can take any hiccups in your stride.

Dealing with distractions

Common distractions can be clinking of cups and glasses when refreshments are brought into the back of the room while you are still presenting. This is a typical scenario for workplace seminars where there is a networking session tagged on at the end or there is a scheduled refreshment break. Other common interruptions can be someone coming in late, phones ringing, doors banging etc.

How you deal with this is important. The audience will take their cue from you – they will focus on wherever your attention goes. If you don't draw attention to it and carry on, then it's no big deal. However if you let these sorts of things stop you in your tracks then the audience starts to look around for the cause of the disruption and then you have lost them. This is why practice is so important; hopefully you will be so well prepared that any disruptions won't throw you off course. I like to think of preparation and rehearsal as pressure proofing – when you spend time building muscle memory in your preparation by rehearsing out loud and becoming familiar with your content, you can always find your place again after being interrupted.

When something potentially distracting happens, take a moment to pause and then carry on. Take a quick look at your notes or mind map if you need to; no one will really notice. If the disruption is quite obvious then perhaps just acknowledge it by referring to it briefly rather than ignoring it – you want to appear responsive and in control, rather than oblivious – and then carry on with your presentation.

Adjustments to timing

Your preparation will have set you up quite well in terms of timing your presentation to fit the slot allocated to you. However things can change at the last minute – in a meeting or conference, for example, you might be told at very short notice to cut your talk or extend it because someone else on the meeting agenda has dropped out. More often than not it will be the former.

In an interview or assessment situation you may be given unexpected last minute changes to test your ability to think on your feet – this simulates real life situations, and one of the most common requests that I get from employers is to train their staff to be able to adapt to this type of challenge. Things change all the time and the ability to confidently adapt is a key skill employers look for.

In earlier chapters we looked at rehearsing your presentation so that you become very familiar with timings of each section. If you have stories that you have refined that now form part of your story collection, you will know how long each one will take. The benefit of this type of preparation really pays off when you are under the pressure of being asked to cut your talk at short notice, because you need to be able to mentally trim sections that are not crucial and yet still be able to get your message across. If I have to do this and I have even a couple of minutes before the meeting starts, I take out my blueprint which highlights all the segments of my talk and then cross bits out. I keep the amended version nearby just in case so that I can glance at it and keep to the new format.

Handling heckling and criticism

I wouldn't suggest that you make an assumption that there will be someone in your audience who is on a mission to derail your presentation but it is good practice to anticipate potential hecklers and plan for it. When you get up to speak, remember the stage is yours. You get to control the space for a short space of time and if you approach it that way you'll be able to confidently deal with any adverse comments that might interrupt your flow. To manage expectations, it can be a good idea to tell your audience at the beginning of your presentation, how you will deal with any questions. We'll look at answering questions on the spot in a later chapter but if you are interrupted by a question then you have a choice. Let them know that if they do have any comments or questions as you are speaking, to make a note so that you can respond to them at the end. That way people are less inclined to interrupt. If you feel confident enough to answer questions and still be able to find your place then tell them you are happy to be interrupted.

In an interview or assessment centre situation, you may well get interrupted by questions. What is being tested is your ability to cope under pressure. Can you deal with it in a professional and confident manner? As in a professional environment, whether you answer the question in that moment or state that you'll come back to it is not the point: how you deal with it is. Keep your composure – rely on your preparation to keep you grounded.

What about if someone in the audience says they've heard 'it' (as in your content) before or they strongly disagree with your opinion? Being able to deal with this is something that comes with experience and practice. The key thing is to be respectful, listen carefully and find a way to take the comments as a form of feedback – remembering that feedback is something to consider and reflect on, rather than take on board with no filter! Don't let it phase you, but do think about their perspective, because it may uncover an angle you hadn't thought of before. The best way to prepare for these types of unexpected comments is to brainstorm them by putting yourself in their shoes. When you are at the research phase, collecting ideas and creating a mind map, make sure you add in a section for objections. Think about all the possible objections that could come up around your topic or related areas and then sketch out some ways in which you might respond.

I sometimes encounter this when I teach workshops on the topic of leadership. Occasionally I'll get a delegate disagreeing with a particular theory I've shared. They might say that it doesn't apply to their department or they've tried it before and it didn't work or that they believe that there are other better theories. In those situations, I acknowledge their viewpoint and accept there might be other ways of looking at it. I don't make them wrong or say that I agree when I don't, but I try to find a way to respectfully take their point on board and then move on with my content.

You want to avoid getting into a heated discussion in front of a room full of other people as well as keep on track with your presentation. Think about some ways you can address uninvited comments respectfully, for example:

'That's an interesting point – I hadn't thought of it that way...'
'Thank you for that... I'll take it on board...'
'Can we pick up on that point at the end of my presentation...?'

Spend some time coming up with a variety of similar phrases that sound right for you and can act as a get out clause in the heat of the moment.

EXERCISE

The best way to learn how to build your resistance muscle in testing situations is to practice. Find a 10-15 minute presentation that you can deliver (with or without slides) and ask a couple of colleagues or friends to be your audience. Tell them to interrupt you and come up with really challenging questions as you deliver your presentation and see how you handle it. It can be really beneficial to get their feedback on how you coped as well as reflecting on your own performance. The more you test yourself the more resilient you will be when it matters.

As with earlier chapters covering the value of preparation and rehearsal, my advice to you is that your success lies in advance planning!

TOP TIPS

- Take a look at the room in advance or try to find out about it if you can.
- Check the AV facilities including sound for playing video clips and an internet connection if you need it.
- Always have your slides saved on a memory stick as a back-up.
- Have a clean version of your mind map or note cards to keep you on track in case your slides fail or you lose your place.
- Pack spare batteries, cables and pens.
- Brainstorm all possible objections to your presentation topic so that you can come up with appropriate responses when under pressure.

17

TAILORING YOUR PRESENTATION TO YOUR AUDIENCE

For your presentation to be effective you want to find where *your* needs (getting your points across, for example) overlap with benefiting your audience – addressing 'WIIFM' (what's in it for me ie *them*). In order to do this you need to have an understanding of what it's like to be in someone else's shoes so that you can meet them where they are and communicate in a way that they will respond to. In other words it helps to be in rapport with or on the same wavelength as your audience so that you can tailor your message and form a better connection with them by paying attention to their specific interests.

An ability to create such a connection will make you more persuasive, more interesting to listen to and more memorable. In your professional career this will give you a competitive edge.

When you have worked with someone for a while, your colleagues, for example, or existing clients, you will have access to much more information about your audience built up over time. Of course, you won't always be presenting to people you know and may have a limited amount of information about your audience. This will definitely be the case when you are presenting as part of a job interview process and quite often in your professional role too – such as presenting to potential clients.

How *can* you build rapport quickly when you are just about to meet a group of people for the first time?

In this chapter I want to share some of my experiences of NLP (neurolinguistic programming) to help you understand how to create better rapport. What is NLP? It is essentially a collection of techniques one can use to better understand our own thought processes and behaviours as well as those of others. There are a huge variety of books and resources you can access to understand this topic in much more detail if you find it of interest. Some books that I have found very useful are:

NLP at Work, Sue Knight
NLP for Dummies, Romilly Ready and Kate Burton
Introducing NLP, Joseph O'Connor and John Seymour

However, rather than get stuck into detailed terminology or techniques, I will give you some simple ideas that will help you better connect with any audience using awareness of sensory learning and chunking of information from big picture to specific details.

Who is your audience – a recap

Before I do that, let's recap some of the ideas covered earlier in the book about researching your audience. Before looking at *how* you can tailor your content you need to have a good idea about who will be your audience and what their level of interest is – who you're tailoring your content to.

Who will be in the audience

Before you start preparing your content, think about why the audience is there and what they want to get out of it. Consider how you can get them on board by making your talk relevant to them. Here are some questions to ask yourself before you begin:

- Who will be there – consider their role, seniority, current knowledge?
- How many people are likely to be there?
- What are they expecting by listening to you?
- Will they expect use of technical or industry terms?
- What questions are they likely to ask?
- What will they want to get from your presentation?

These are aspects to consider when preparing for almost all types of presentations. In Chapter 3 we covered all the different scenarios in which your presentation skills might be put to the test from participating in team meetings to speaking at industry conferences as a subject area expert. When it comes to interview and assessment centre presentations however, there are a few other aspects to take into account as discussed in Chapter 2. You still need to go over the above list to form a picture of the type of characters you have in your audience but the interview panel are looking out for evidence of certain skillsets in addition to you being able build rapport and provide value.

They will be looking for evidence of confidently:

- Structuring content in a logical manner
- Adequate knowledge of the company and role through prior research
- Tailoring content to serve the audience's expectations or fit the brief
- Ability to speak for the allocated amount of time
- Flexibility in dealing with interruptions and answering questions
- Audience engagement through eye contact and non verbal cues

Once you have clarity about your audience's needs, you can refine the objectives of your presentation.

Researching material to interest your audience

The most important factor to consider in any presentation is your audience – that's why it's so beneficial to go over the checklists in the section above to analyse what their expectations might be before tailoring content to match that. In Chapter 4, I made some suggestions as to how to gather material to help you with finding interesting content in your presentations. When you are focusing on tailoring that content to your target audience you want to keep thinking about what matters to *them* as you gather information and start constructing your talk.

For example, if there are important developments in the industry, what articles can you access through online news sites or social media platforms that your audience might be reading? When presenting at an interview, what information can you gather about the company that you can weave into your content to show you have taken the time to carry out your research?

The same concept applies to finding interesting stories or case studies to bring in – which ones will resonate best with them? The next time you are preparing for a presentation go back over Chapter 4 to review ideas for sourcing material and then as you begin to select examples, data or stories pick the ones that will connect best with your audience.

Preferences in processing information using our senses

A few years ago I worked with pupils at a high school providing one to one coaching sessions on leadership and personal development. During one of those coaching sessions, I noticed that the student had a folder with a big letter 'V' written on the front cover. When I asked what it meant, she told me it was there to alert the teacher in the classroom as to her preferred way of receiving information – 'V' meant she was a visual learner. Similarly other students had 'A' for auditory or 'K' for kinaesthetic (sometimes referred to as *feelings*) to represent the three aspects of the VAK learning styles or preferred system of processing information.

This VAK preferred system is popular with teachers and trainers. In theory, most of us prefer to learn or take in information in one of three ways. Many of the NLP techniques focused around better communication refer to this concept of the VAK preferred input system, which says that as we go about our everyday lives, we naturally access all of our senses, however we tend to filter reality in one of these three main ways. All of the above recommended books discuss this concept in great detail – *Introducing NLP* by Joseph O'Connor and John Seymour explains it really well. As we become aware of how we think and make sense of the world, we can better understand how to connect with others. Not everybody thinks like you of course.

Awareness of learning styles in schools is relatively high as in the above example, but it isn't something that has made it's way into the workplace and yet we process information all the time. This is just one approach to learning styles, there are others but I like referring to this one as it's so simple and easy to follow. When we interact with the world around us, we do so in unique ways. Let me give you an overview of how this works:

Visual – is what we see

Someone with a dominant visual preference retains information better when it's presented in images. Use of graphs, diagrams or pictures works for this group. When learning something new, this group likes to follow written instructions or watch someone else go through the process first. Want to be shown rather than told.

Auditory – is what we hear

A learner with a dominant auditory preference likes to listen. They prefer verbal presentations and discussions – storytelling is a very powerful way to engage this group. Unlike the visual group, these people are happy to receive verbal instructions in person or over the telephone and can remember them. Asking the audience to discuss a question in pairs or mini groups is a good way to engage this group. They want to be told rather than shown.

Kinaesthetic – is what we do or feel

A kinaesthetic learner has a preference for connecting with the emotional aspect of a situation or a physical experience such as an activity or handling a prop. They like to experiment using trial and error to figure something out and probably don't look at instructions beforehand! You might want to include team activities or some form of active exploration for example, being able to physically hold a sample or prototype. They want to be doing – not to be told or shown.

This insight can be really beneficial in helping you think how best to adapt your content so that you put it across in a way that someone prefers to receive it. You can't of course, tailor your content to each individual in a mixed group – unlike the letters marked on the folders in my case study above, you won't have that sort of information unless of course you know the people in your audience quite well. What you can do is provide material in a variety of formats – a multi sensory approach. There will be mix of preferences in any typical audience – some people are more visual than others. Some can't sit still for too long without interaction to keep them engaged. When you are designing your talk, remember to use a variety of formats such as powerful images, storytelling and audience participation. I'll cover ideas for audience interaction in Chapter 20 later.

Having an understanding of these sensory preferences will help you tailor your content or message for any type of communication from formal presentations to effectively delegating tasks to your team. It is important to note that while we do have a preference for processing information with one sense in particular, we do all have a mix of preferences and they do change from one situation to another.

For example I am an auditory learner. I enjoy sitting in seminars and listening to thought leaders. When I am travelling on a train, I'll listen to podcasts rather than read books as listening is my preferred medium for taking in information. I love to read as well but listening is easier for me. However when I am searching for directions to reach a new destination, I use a variety of senses. First, I will look up the map on Google Maps so that I have a visual representation – I'll even look at the street view photographic display to look for landmarks and shop fronts which all help me to visualize the landscape. Then I will print the map with written directions so that have something tangible to hold in my hand as I am walking to my destination. When I am on route I'll often ask a passer by if I am going in the right direction for added confirmation! Utilizing all three senses (VAK) creates a richer experience for me. If I were to just rely on oral directions without sight of a map then I would feel much less confident about my ability to find the right address – that's just me. The same is true for my car journeys. – the verbal directions on my SatNav are usually very clear and appropriately paced just ahead of when action is required from me but I still need to look at the coloured screen sitting on my dashboard to bolster my confidence in the information being shared. My preferred medium is auditory and yet when it comes to directions, I need visual content as well. Sometimes I walk around until I work out where I am by trial and error.

EXERCISE

What is your preferred style? You won't only have one preferred style all the time but when you start paying attention to how you interact with the world around you, you'll begin to notice if you have a stronger preference for one of the senses. Think about how you navigate through different situations:

For example, how do you respond to a challenge? Do you brainstorm and plan it out visually, talk to someone to bounce off ideas or try it out to test?

If you are given a task, do you need to see a demonstration, see a diagram or written instructions or will just listening to verbal instructions be enough for you to grasp what is required?

What about when you are sitting in a presentation or meeting? Do you need visuals such as slides handouts to help you get the picture or are you happy just listening?

Think back to the last time you had dinner with a group of friends – what do you remember the best? Is it the sounds, the atmosphere and smells or what you saw?

Do you notice a pattern or a preference in your responses to these examples?

To find out where your preferences lie, why not take a quick test? There are plenty of free online tests available – just Google 'preferred VAK learning styles test' and answer the range of questions to give you an insight into how you like to process information!

Using language deliberately to better connect with your audience

In addition to adapting your content, you can also be a little more deliberate about the way you describe things – with multi-sensory language. You can identify someone's preference for handling information through the sensory language they use in every day communication.

Here are some examples of words or phrases that you may hear each group use:

Visual Learners

Words such as: see, look, imagine
Phrases such as:
Can you see what I mean?
Do you get the picture?
It appears as if…

Auditory Learners

Words such as: listen, hear, sound, resonate

Phrases such as:

    Does that sound right?

    This might strike a chord…

    It's as clear as a bell

Kinaesthetic Learners

Words such as: do, feel, get

Phrases such as:

    Does that feel right?

    Would you like to try it?

    Help you get to grips with…

The way to create rapport with a mixed group of people is to use a selection of the different sensory words and phrases during your presentation. This can also be really helpful in creating better working relationships when you are communicating with managers or other team members – you can speak their language!

Another way to tailor your content with words is to incorporate buzz words or industry terms that the audience will be familiar with. When you are in the preparation stage of your presentation, look for words or phrases that resonate with your target audience and think about how you can insert a few of those into your material. It's about balance – you don't want to overload them with jargon or acronyms because the best way to engage others is to use everyday language and have a conversational style. Cramming in too many buzzwords will detract from the clarity of your message and makes you sound less authentic.

EXERCISE

Watch some of the TED talks I have listed in this book and listen carefully to what sensory language the speakers use. Keep a tally chart in front of you with three separate columns for visual, auditory and kinaesthetic and put a marker whenever you hear relevant words or phrases. You'll notice that one column might have more markers in it than the other two which will give you a clue as to how that speaker prefers to communicate.

By doing this exercise a few times, you'll be able to sharpen your listening skills and easily spot cues in other peoples' language that you can respond to.

Chunking or sizing your information to suit your audience

In a similar way to having a preference as to which senses we use in processing information, we also have a preference for how much detail we can or want to cope with at any given time. When receiving instructions for a task or becoming involved in a project, some people need an overview first before the nitty gritty otherwise they struggle to find context. Others are completely opposite – they want all the details first; that's their way of putting a situation into context.

Chunking of information like this is another NLP concept. Chunk size refers to the scale or amount of information someone prefers to work with in order to understand a concept or task. Think of a sliding scale – at one end the smallest block would be very detailed, at the other end the biggest block would relate to the headlines or overview.

This is very useful when negotiating. Getting bogged down in detail prevents parties from reaching an agreement. Focusing on the bigger picture rather than arguing over small points moves the conversation towards reaching a consensus. It can be difficult to reach decisions when people focus on the smaller details. By chunking up you can find common ground and areas of agreement. Even in everyday workplace interactions, where there is a mismatch of preferences, there is no rapport and can lead to misunderstanding and frustration. When in doubt, you can ask the other person what their preference is. Big picture or minute detail. Abstract or detailed road map.

How is this relevant to presentations? You might end up giving someone too much detail and they begin to lose interest. Or in contrast you give only the general background and that is not enough detail for someone who needs the nitty gritty step by step details to fully understand what is involved. Ideally you want to be able to slide up and down this scale to adapt to your audience and be flexible. Give an overview of the topic before launching into specifics. Otherwise you risk your audience becoming impatient with all the details because they cannot put it into context that is meaningful to them. This ties in with WIIFM – addressing the *why* – in Chapter 5 I suggested ordering your content by starting your presentation with this.

As with any of these concepts, this is not about putting people in boxes or categories. The idea is to get some insight into preferences, become more conscious of how people communicate so that we have a choice to as to how to adapt our own approach.

The suggestions I've made about how to build rapport quickly would apply not just to presentation settings, but all manner of situations where you have to interact with others. This is really useful for persuading others in your role at work as well as making connections when you are networking.

TOP TIPS

- Take time to analyse who will be in your audience even if you have never met them before – make an educated guess of what their motivation is.

- When you have an outline for your talk, go back over it to find ways to adapt your content by utilizing VAK or chunking and link it to your target audience.

- Give yourself a challenge once a week to listen out for VAK language patterns either at work or outside so that you get better at spotting preferences.

18

IMPRESSING POTENTIAL EMPLOYERS IN AN INTERVIEW PRESENTATION

In this book there are dedicated chapters covering all aspects of presentation skills – ranging from the importance of mastering such skills for your career to techniques for better audience engagement. Each of these areas apply to presentations in many different situations. This chapter however focuses on a slightly different type – it is specifically designed to be a standalone quick reference guide covering everything you need to prepare for a presentation as part of a job interview process. You can always refer back to earlier chapters on specific topics for more background later. Let's go through the key elements to get you ready for that all important interview presentation.

Clarify the brief and find out what's expected

When you receive details about your interview, you'll get some information about the presentation slot as well. You will typically be given the topic you are required to speak about as well as how long you are expected to speak for. Generally the topic will be related to the area of work you are applying to be part of to simulate a real life scenario. It may also be possible that you won't have any advance notice of your topic because it will be given to you when you arrive for your interview and you'll have a short amount of time to prepare something. I'll talk about that scenario a little later.

Make sure that you have as much information as possible so that you can properly plan. If you feel there is not enough detail within your instructions, don't be shy about contacting your prospective employer to clarify anything. The worst that can happen is that you may not receive a reply, but by double checking you minimize any uncertainty or risk of going off track. You will also demonstrate that you're thorough and attention to detail is important to you. If you don't get a reply the first time you ask, you may want to follow up again with a gentle reminder – things get missed because people are busy or your original email might have gone into a spam folder perhaps. If for some reason you don't get the clarification you want, you will have to prepare without it and make an educated guess. Here are some possible areas you might want to check:

- Are you required to use slides?
- Will you need to bring any slides on a memory stick or send them via email?
- Will there be a remote clicker, flip chart or other resources in the room?
- Who and how many people will be on the panel, what are their roles?
- Do you need to tailor your content for a specific type of audience?

This last point refers to the situation where the panel might like you to pretend they are a particular type of audience, for example one of their clients. If that is the case, you will need to take this into consideration and adapt your presentation for the benefit of the imaginary audience.

Research your audience and topic

As we have seen in previous chapters, to deliver a successful presentation in any context, you need to determine what your audience actually wants. Before you can do that, you have to carry out some research. For an interview or assessment centre scenario, this research is quite specific. If you have been advised of the names of your interview panel then you can look those members up on the company website and sites like LinkedIn. Get to know them as best as you can – what are their roles and responsibilities? Is there any information about their professional background that can give you clues about their interests? If you know anyone already working for that organization, see if you can ask them what they know. Going through this investigation stage will really help you structure your presentation in a way that will engage the panel. Remember, the topic doesn't mean much on its own without you bringing it to life and adapting it for each person in your audience.

Similarly, find out as much as you can about the given topic. A good starting place is the company website – check if they have written any articles or blogs or shared anything on social media platforms. Have a wider look at information on the internet that competitors or other institutions have shared as well as books and podcasts. Find out about key trends as well as areas of concern for the industry and company itself. Make notes as you carry out this research so that you can easily access it when you get to the structuring phase of your presentation as you might want to include key points. Those notes will also be useful as a quick reference guide to help you prepare for answering questions on the spot. Having this type of information at your fingertips will bolster your credibility and showcase your level of preparation.

EXERCISE

Set aside one hour when you won't be distracted. Identify three companies in your industry sector (including your current organization if appropriate). For each of those companies – analyse all pages on their websites and social media platforms and start making notes about how they conduct business, what pressures they face, opportunities to innovate or grow etc. After an hour, you'll probably be surprised about how much you've gathered by way of background research. Obviously you can spent more time doing this if you have it. By picking a few companies at a time, you can identify trends and common issues as well as what might differentiate them from each other. You weave this information into your presentation to make it more relevant and personal to the panel.

Structure your material for the benefit of the interview panel

The likelihood is that the total time slot for your presentation will be about 10 minutes. You will inevitably have much more raw material about your topic than you can possibly fit into your time slot. Once you have gathered that raw material through your research, it's time to structure your presentation around a few well chosen points. Keep your structure simple and clear. Remember to keep to about 3 main points in total. The reason for this is that typically we can only consciously retain between 3 – 5 bits of information. There is a more detailed discussion about this in Chapter 5. Your presentation needs to focus on quality rather than quantity – it's always tempting to cram in everything you know about a subject but this doesn't serve your audience. Think about the purpose of your presentation – what is it that you want the audience to do or think by the time you get to the end of your talk? Be ruthless about how much content you include – only add in enough to build a logical path from your introduction to your closing remarks.

You should have some insight into the areas of interests for the panel members – use that to help you choose the points you want to make. Think about stories, case studies or anecdotes that fit well with the culture of the company or specific interests for the panel – they will help make your content more engaging and memorable. More importantly, it will make *you* more memorable.

Craft strong openings and endings to create impact

The beginning and end of presentations tend to be the ones that people remember the most. The beginning because it's what grabs their attention and the end because it's the last part they hear. Think of those aspects of your presentation as book ends.

When it comes to planning a presentation, I always recommend working on the ending first. When you are clear about what you want the audience to do or think about by the time you are finished, the rest of your talk is easier to craft. Close with a strong clear conclusion – either a call to action or summary of your main points.

You also want to find a way to engage the panel really quickly so they look forward to the rest of your talk. It's highly likely that they will have sat through several versions of that presentation from other candidates that day – what will make yours stand out? Not only do you want your message or key takeaway to be memorable, but you also want the interviewers to be left with a good impression of you – will you be a good fit for their company? A typical tactic is to open with a brief overview of what you will cover – what your presentation is about. There is nothing wrong with this as it sets the scene, however I'd encourage you to use your imagination and find ways in which to motivate your audience to want to sit there and listen to you. Can you find a shocking fact or example to open with? Whatever you choose, remember you are setting the scene as well as answering the 'what's in it for me?' question for your interviewers.

Visual content to bring your presentation to life

When we think of visual content in workplace presentations, we automatically assume this means slides. Not necessarily – it may be that use of slides has been requested by the panel, but if not think about how else you can bring in visual content. Sometimes, not using slides at all can be really refreshing and unexpected for the panel. Can you use a prop or handouts instead? Your decision as to what to use should be based on whether it enhances your point and helps the audience process what you are sharing. Visual representations can help an audience's understanding of a concept. Don't use slides just for the sake of it. Remember, when choosing what to put into your slides consider: do they add impact by clarifying a point or making it simpler?

If slides are the main visual element you will be using, then remember they are your support act – you are the presentation! Create stunning yet simple slides. Keep away from text heavy slides and opt for images or graphics that are clear and easy to interpret. Graphs or flow charts can help illustrate numbers or trends in a clearer way than listing the data as bullet points. Sometimes, all you need is an interesting picture or infographic that appears in the background as you talk about the point your making. What you definitely want to avoid is putting text on the slide and then repeating exactly what you have on it. The slide is there to be a hook or reference point to help increase the audience experience; *you* are the presentation not the slide deck!

When sourcing images, look for good quality pictures that won't look distorted when projected on a big screen. Keep the slides clutter free – especially when you are displaying text. Rather than long sentences, use key points so that you can talk around them rather than expect the audience to read your slide. Choose fonts and colours that are easy to read from a distance. You won't know what the lighting will be like in the presentation room – there could be bright sunshine coming through a window that could ruin the contrast and make it difficult to see your slides. Choose dark font colours on white or light backgrounds to avoid this happening.

You can also think about using handouts. Sometimes this can be really helpful to show more detailed information or graphs. Take enough copies so you have enough for every panel member.

What to do when you aren't given a topic in advance

So far we've made the assumption that you have advance knowledge of the topic you will be speaking about. There are some interview situations where you only find out what the topic is on the actual day of your interview. You are then given a short amount of time to prepare. This tactic is adopted to test how you perform under pressure and adapt at short notice. You can still prepare for this scenario. All the advice for researching your audience is relevant, as is looking for articles and news items that are topical. By looking at the company website and the job description you have applied for, you should be able to make an educated guess as to the types of topics that might come up. In a way it's like revising for a school exam – you have the entire syllabus to cover and will only be asked a selection of questions on the day because you can't possibly be tested on everything. How familiar you are with your subject area or industry sector in this case, will directly influence how easy you'll find scoping out a presentation at short notice.

When the actual topic is revealed and you sit down to plan your content, stick to the following outline:

- Opening – something to set the scene and grab attention
- Main section or body – 3 key points that flow in a logical sequence
- Closing – summarize the main points and conclude with a call to action or recommendation.

Resist spending the entire preparation time allowed just writing out your script. Instead spend a maximum of two thirds of the time on structuring your key points and the rest on rehearsing your opening and closing lines. Even if you have nowhere quiet to go and rehearse out loud, run it over in your mind. Learning your opening line will give you confidence. Tidy up your notes so that you can easily refer to them if you need to during your presentation.

What other skills are they looking for?

Unless you are interviewing for a role as a full time trainer or speaker, the presentation task is there to test more than just the quality of the presentation itself.

Here are some aspects that panels usually look for:

- Ability to communicate with clarity
- Ability to engage an audience
- The quality of your ideas or thought process
- How you cope under pressure
- organizational skills – how prepared you are beforehand and whether you can stick to the allotted time

Think about how you can demonstrate these skills as you are presenting. All the TED talks I've referenced in this book are engaging because they use storytelling – my favorite example is Ken Robinson's talk, which has short anecdotes well told. By incorporating stories or case studies in your presentation you will demonstrate that you have focused on the audience experience. By finishing your presentation within the allotted time without rushing, demonstrates good organizational skills.

Your delivery style

I've said this before – content is important but the way you share it is more important, especially in an interview situation. This is the opportunity to show the panel your personality through your delivery – keep it natural and conversational and be enthusiastic about your topic. There is an entire section with tips on engaging delivery in Chapter 13 about body language. However, for an interview, the key points to think about are:

- Speak slower than usual – adrenalin can cause you to speed up and sound nervous
- Keep a balanced posture and avoid distracting gestures or fidgeting
- Maintain consistent eye contact and avoid looking at the screen or the floor
- Relaxed facial expressions and smiling when appropriate make a big difference
- Pause at key points to allow the audience time to process
- Use vocal variety to avoid sounding monotonous

Learn your material well and prepare user-friendly notes

I can't emphasize enough how beneficial it is to be as well prepared as you can. You want to be a in a position where you know your content inside out and can just concentrate on being present in the moment, focusing on creating rapport with the panel. If you want to see how people can get flustered and trip up in front of a panel, have a look at some examples of either *Dragons' Den* (BBC2 – in the UK) or *Shark Tank* (USA). Both of these TV shows work on the basis that companies needing investment and guidance from successful business owners will come and pitch their ideas to a panel of five such individuals. Each member of the panel is looking for companies with potential to invest in. The pitch lasts for a few minutes and then the floor is open for the panel to ask questions. What is quite shocking is that many people consistently get caught out when asked about basic financial information about their company. Of course, not everyone is an expert in accounting but if you are going in to ask for investment of several thousand pounds or dollars, you better be prepared to know your stuff. If you appear vague or not credible, no one will want to part with their money and take a risk with you. The format of this show has not changed in many years – it would be really easy to watch a few episodes of the show to know what the investors are looking for. Then all you have to do is prepare your answers – but this little insight has escaped many budding entrepreneurs and they end up walking away with no deal. In fact if you look up clips on Youtube you'll be able to see how little preparation they put into their pitch.

In your interview presentation you are also asking for an investment – not in your company but in yourself as a valuable addition to the team. Set yourself up for success and learn your material. If you can't do that because you haven't been given your topic yet, learn as much as you can about the trends and issues of concern for the company as mentioned above. You may also need to have some notes to use as a prompt if you haven't had the luxury of preparing in advance. Make sure that you write bullet points or key words that are large enough so that you can find what you need quickly. Take along some blank notecards that you can fill in as you plan your presentation, or draw out a mind map if you prefer to do that. It doesn't matter that you might need notes for quick reference, what matters is that you use something that is easily accessible for you and that does not get in the way of you being able to maintain eye contact with the panel.

Pressure proof your presentation with rehearsal

If you can, test your presentation out in front of colleagues or friends. That way you can get views on what works and what could be improved. They will also be able to give you feedback on any annoying distractions or content that is not as clear as it could be. Ask them to give you specific feedback as to whether you sound like your normal self because that's what you want to aim for. Even if you can't find anyone to practise in front of, rehearse on your own and speak out loud so that you can hear what the content sounds like. Better still, record it – that is the best test. Rehearsing will help you get more familiar with your content, keep to your allowed time slot and help you with your confidence. Rehearsing like this will give you a good foundation so that even if something unexpected happens on the day like an interruption from the panel, you can still find your place and pick up where you left off.

Taking control of your mindset

Much of the focus in this chapter has been about preparation of the presentation itself. We need to also consider preparing *you* – your mindset and beliefs.

It is quite common to feel some level of anxiety about standing up and speaking to a group of strangers. In addition you may feel some pressure by focusing on the thought that the success of the presentation is directly linked to the job offer. Typical thoughts that may be going through your mind:

- What if I freeze and my mind goes blank?

- They won't be interested in this topic and will be bored
- I'll look stupid if I don't have the right answers

It's much more helpful to shift any self talk to:

- There is no such thing as failure, only feedback – I can treat this as a learning experience
- There are no boring topics, only boring presenters
- The more I prepare, the better I become – I know my stuff and can make my presentation interesting for them
- It's fine to not know all the answers – I can confidently say I don't know but can find out later
- I can look at my notes if I need to

We get what we focus on – if you keep thinking about what might go wrong then it can become a downward spiral. Every time you catch yourself thinking negative unhelpful thoughts, make an effort to think of something more helpful such as how much preparation you have done already or that you have your notes in your pocket if you need them – things that you can control.

Visualization is another technique that is really powerful for feeling confident and getting into the right mindset – in a similar way to consciously shifting your focus away from negative thoughts to more positive ones. Imagine your presentation going exactly the way you want it to. It's like a movie that you play in your mind, except you get to decide how to play it. Choose the scenario as you want it to be. Imagine you are in front of the panel having prepared really well. What do you see happening – what's happening with your posture, face, gestures? What do you hear – the tone of your voice and the pace, are you speaking clearly and slowly? Imagine the audience hanging on your every word, looking interested in your presentation and nodding approval. There is a step by step visualization exercise in Chapter 12 that you might find helpful to go through.

To bring it all together – the way in which you can impress employers in an interview presentation is to ensure your level of preparation is as high as it can be. Spend time identifying your audience and researching what will be of interest to them. The quality of your presentation will showcase your willingness to go above and beyond and demonstrate your commitment. Devote time to rehearsal and testing out your presentation so that you can be your best self when under pressure in front of the panel.

TOP TIPS

- Take the time to research your audience so that you can find ways to engage with them in the presentation by adapting your content and style to match.

- Make sure you test your presentation before you have to deliver it for real – it's better to make mistakes in rehearsal!

- Watch video clips of entrepreneurial pitches on shows such as Dragon's Den or Shark Tank to see how the panel are adversely influenced by candidates that are underprepared so that you know what to avoid.

19

ANSWERING QUESTIONS ON THE SPOT

You've prepared for your presentation – devoting hours in refining your content and rehearsing your delivery. When it comes to the day of your presentation, you've delivered it well – calmly and confidently…and then come the dreaded questions! If handled well, the question segment puts you in an even better position by consolidating what you've shared as well as putting you in a good light as someone who is confident and competent. If handled badly it can derail your entire presentation, knock your confidence and possibly damage your credibility. Being able to deal with questions on the spot professionally and effectively will help you stand apart from other speakers. It's not just about knowing the answers, it's about how you handle yourself and interact with your audience.

Being asked to answer questions on the spot can come up in lots of different workplace scenarios. The two main cases that we will focus on in this chapter are presentations within an interview or assessment process as well as seminar type presentations. You can always expect to be asked questions after your presentation slot in a recruitment situation because the panel will be looking for a range of skill sets including the ability to think on your feet, whereas when you deliver a presentation at a client seminar or conference for example, you will be asked questions by the audience for their own benefit – either to clarify a point or ask about something related to your topic that you didn't cover but could possibly shed some light on. The tips and techniques I'll share with you here are relevant to both these types of scenarios but are also useful when:

- Put on the spot in internal meetings after you've provided a team update
- Asking for approval for a project from senior managers or the Board of Directors

- Facilitating a training workshop
- Pitching to new clients or customers

Whatever the case, you want to aim to stay in control. Treat questions as part of the presentation – they require as much careful planning as the main content of your talk. Something that I cannot emphasize enough: Prepare. Prepare. Prepare.

Why you shouldn't dread questions

Many otherwise confident speakers will admit that they dread the question and answer section because they feel they might lose control of the presentation. They fear that they will be caught out and asked questions they are not prepared for or simply cannot answer, which might make them look incompetent in some way. However, rather than being fearful of questions, think of them as an opportunity to add even more value to your audience by giving people the chance to clarify points and consolidate learning for the wider audience. When your audience asks questions, it shows they are still engaged and are interested to know more. By serving them in this way, you also have the chance to build trust and credibility for both yourself and your company.

Planning ahead – brainstorming and rehearsing

Great presenters plan for questions by predicting what is likely to come up. You might be thinking how this can be possible? Well, in the same way that you need to put yourself in the shoes of your audience when honing your content to meet their area of interest, you need to do the same when brainstorming questions they may have. The background research and work you've put in already to finalize your presentation should set you up quite well to be able to handle questions connected to your topic. You will have gathered a lot more raw material than you could possibly insert into your talk – that foundation of knowledge base is not wasted. For example you might have collected a number of research studies but only decided to include one or two key facts from them in your presentation. You'll have the information at your fingertips should someone ask you to expand upon what you covered in your talk.

Think about every single person in your audience, even if you don't know them personally. Look back at Chapter 18 to review the section about identifying the members in your audience; this will help you frame your answer to meet their needs more specifically. What might they want to know? Will they challenge your views and ask if you have any further material to support your opinion? Perhaps they'll ask what could go wrong – for example, if you are presenting about a new product or way of working. No question you come up with is ridiculous at this point – you are pressure testing your bank of knowledge or expertise in a particular area. Prepare some adaptable answers as part of your content development phase. Thinking about your talk in this way will help you develop a deeper understanding or gain a better insight. You might want to try organizing your questions into groups around your key points and write them out on separate cards that you can carry around with you to keep looking over in the days before your presentation.

For an interview based presentation, remember it's not just clarification of your material that the panel will be seeking. They'll come up with questions designed to challenge you and see how cope under pressure.

Once you've brainstormed all possible questions it's a good idea to rehearse what you will say in response:

EXERCISE

A great way to practise fielding questions is to rehearse your presentation in front of colleagues as suggested in Chapter 4; always make time for the opportunity to rehearse any presentation in front of others whose opinion you trust. Do the same thing with your list of possible questions that you think may come up after your presentation. It's as if you are revising for an exam and you don't know exactly which questions will be asked but you need to be familiar with your entire course content for the year. Practise answering these questions and ask for feedback from your audience – did you answer the actual question succinctly or did you waffle? Did your voice and body language convey confidence in the same way as in the main presentation? If not what could you adjust?

The final point I'd like to make in terms of advance preparation is about timing. You need to build in time to allow for questions and test this out in your rehearsal. For example if you are given 20 minutes for your presentation, aim to speak for 15 minutes to allow the remaining 5 minutes for questions. Even if the audience sit there in stunned silence and don't ask you anything, you can still fill that time by covering one or two extra points. I'll talk about this more in the next chapter, but if you have asked if there are any questions and no one says anything, rather than ending on a flat note you can include a final point...'I often get asked...' If you are given a specific time slot by a potential employer in advance of an interview or attending an assessment centre, then assume that you will be required to speak for the entire time slot and questions will be asked *after* you finish. If in doubt about timings, always check in advance.

Setting ground rules for tackling questions

Now that you have planned and rehearsed for questions, let's focus on how to deal with them when you are actually standing at the front of the room in the spotlight. Take the opportunity at the beginning of your talk to clarify when you would prefer to take questions. This is your presentation so you decide what works best:

- Will you answer all questions at the end of your main presentation?
- Are you happy to take questions at anytime as you would rather clear up any issues as you go along?
- Will you pause for questions at the end of each section?

There are no hard and fast rules about how you should decide to incorporate questions, but by giving the audience guidelines you maintain control of your session and it serves as a reminder to get them thinking about any queries which will promote audience interaction. Taking questions during your talk increases engagement and clarifies any misunderstandings as you go along, but on the flip side you can get drawn into a lengthy interaction that could throw you off course and mess up your timings. To avoid this happening, keep an eye on the time and stick to brief answers. If you need more time to expand on your answer say so and perhaps indicate that you will come back to this point when you finish speaking – just make sure you remember to do that. Encourage them to write down any questions that they think of – perhaps provide them with note paper to do so. When you get to towards the end of your presentation, you could say something like:

> 'That's the end of my presentation but I'd like to take questions from the audience...'

Dealing with difficult questions

Sometimes questions are not really straightforward. When you invite people to put their hands up to ask you a question they will have different reasons for doing so. The most straightforward is when someone is seeking clarification about your content. This should be quite simple to respond to and can be useful feedback for you – perhaps next time you may want to include a more detailed explanation. You may get a question about something that is related to a point you will come to later – in that case politely thank the questioner and say you'll pick it up when you get to the relevant section.

Then there are questions that really put you on the spot and the answer doesn't immediately come to mind or it's an aspect you hadn't fully considered before – basically these are what most speakers fear – difficult questions. Relax in the knowledge that you have prepared well and that you cannot know everything – no one can. There are however tactics to help you cope with this situation.

First of all, get clarification so that you are answering the actual question rather than going off on a tangent. Take your time, listen, pause and make sure you fully understand the intention behind the question before launching in with your reply. You don't want to respond with an inaccurate answer – sometimes nerves can influence us and we might not focus clearly under pressure. When an entire audience is watching and listening it can be tempting to jump straight in with an answer. Don't.

Listen to the entire question before formulating your answer without jumping to conclusions – sometimes it won't become completely clear what the person asking the question actually wants to know until the end of their sentence because they are thinking off the top of their heads and might also want to share their opinion on your topic all wrapped up together! This is quite normal by the way – you'll see it happen quite often in seminars when someone is very keen to be heard and get their point across. You could end up going down the wrong path if you home in on key words without properly considering the context of the question in full. Try to understand the intention behind the question:

'Let me check I understand it right – what you are asking is…'
   'So if I understand you correctly, are you saying…'

Don't be afraid to admit you can't answer something if you don't know the answer – much better to say so than bumbling or making it up, they'll be able to tell anyway. Find a way to say *I don't know* but keep positive and be sincere:

'I don't have the exact answer and I don't want to guess…however, I can find out and get back to you later'
   'That's an interesting idea, I hadn't thought of it in that way…'

Keep a written note of the question you couldn't answer as well as how to get in touch with the person who asked so that you can follow up later.

Involving the audience is another option. Turn it into a collaborative effort with you as the facilitator and ask if anyone else can answer or has experience in that area. You are adding value by doing this and showing that you aren't above learning new ideas or admitting you don't know everything. In a work setting, you might have a senior colleague or subject expert in the room who can help you out:

> 'My colleague is more familiar with this area than I am…'

On a general note, I would stay away from saying 'that's a great question…' because unless you say that to all the questioners, others may feel as if their question was not so good and obviously you can't keep saying 'great question' in response to everyone as it can come across as insincere. But it's a matter of personal choice of course – find phrases that you feel comfortable using and that fit the occasion.

Sticking to the issue and not taking comments personally

It's also possible that a questioner may strongly disagree with your viewpoint. It can become quite awkward but you can still deal with this situation respectfully and keep control by firmly acknowledging you each have a different view but you do need to move on either to give others a chance to ask questions or conclude your presentation by moving on to your final point or summary. Focus on the issue at hand rather than feeling defensive. People want to see you keep calm under pressure.

> 'That falls outside of the objectives for today's presentation, but perhaps we can discuss this further later…?'
> 'Thank you for opinion/insights on this…'

Involving the entire audience

Always make sure the entire audience hears the question being asked. Repeat it to the whole room before answering. Remember that even though you are taking a question from one person, you still need to maintain engagement for the rest of the audience. Your response should be addressed to the entire room not just the person who raised the question, otherwise people will start to lose interest and become bored. It's exactly why repeating the question is so important, especially in larger groups where there is no microphone – if they can't hear the question they won't be able to follow along with your interaction. The other thing to bear in mind is that not everyone feels confident enough to put up their hand and speak in front of peers, but someone else may ask a question that they wanted to ask themselves which makes the question and answer session very valuable.

Keeping to the topic and unravelling lots of questions wrapped up together

Just as there are people who feel reluctant to ask a question in front of a room full of people, there are those that love the sound of their own voice or want to publicly share their thoughts. Quite often they will bring up something that is off topic or ask an obscure question that the rest of audience won't be interested in – again thank them for their insights, make a note of anything you may need to follow up with later and firmly state you need to get back to the main presentation or want to give others a chance to ask a question:

'I think we might be going off on a tangent here – let's put that to one side and we can talk about it some more later during the networking session.'

'We don't have enough time to explore that further right now …I'd like to carry on with the presentation otherwise I may not have enough time left to finish, but let's talk about this later.'

In addition to rambling on, you might also get someone asking several questions in one go and it may be tricky to handle this. As before check that you have understood what is being asked by repeating it back. Make notes so that you have a written reference to keep you on track, then decide if you will answer all the questions or deal with the most relevant and agree to come back to the rest another time.

Closing strong and wrapping up the Q and A section

At some point you'll need to end your Q and A session because you have a schedule to stick to – make it clear time is up and keep control of the situation. It's a nice problem to have if you get lots of questions because that's a signal that people are interested and engaged. However, you don't want to end with your Q and A session. Even though you've brainstormed all possible questions, there is still an element of the unknown when tackling questions as you don't know where they'll come from. If the last question is weak or not very interesting perhaps even slightly negative then it can bring the energy of your presentation down. Thank the audience for questions, summarize your main points then end with your rehearsed conclusion.

In Chapter 10 we discussed strong openings and endings and why they are so important. The opening should grab attention and the closing is the last thing the audience hear from you and should leave them thinking about something or enable them to take some kind of action following what you have shared. Finish with closing remarks that will resonate with them.

TOP TIPS

- Take the time to listen to questions before deciding how to answer, pause a moment and take your time before you respond.

- Clearly state your preferred way of dealing with questions by letting the audience know at the beginning of your talk.

- Always include the entire audience in your responses – whether that involves a small panel of interviewers or a larger room full of people.

- Practise ways in which you can respond to awkward questions – be comfortable with your version of 'I don't know'.

- Always frame your responses in a positive way so that the questioner feels respected and not made to feel wrong.

20

AUDIENCE INTERACTION OR PARTICIPATION

One of the biggest challenges faced by speakers in any presentation setting is that of how to connect with the audience. As explored in previous chapters, tailoring your content and delivery to your target audience helps with this. In other words, making sure you think about enhancing their experience and avoid bad habits such as reading from slides or talking at them in a monotone voice. We've all sat through mind-numbing presentations where this sort of thing happens and the speaker just does not engage with the audience. This is the scenario that we've become used to as the common standard for workplace presentations and as an audience member we usually expect to be talked at. Remember also, that it's completely normal for people to zone out and start daydreaming or thinking about something else because we have limited attention spans. Your job as a speaker is to grab their attention and then keep it throughout by stimulating thought and understanding. Don't give them an excuse to take a nap!

Have the audience do something. Through action, people commit new information to memory. Getting active about an idea helps us to remember better or gain more value. The point of a successful presentation is to help the audience utilize what you share. This is where audience interaction or participation comes in: creating rapport through encouraging audience participation will contribute to the success of your presentation.

In this chapter, I'd like to take you through different levels of audience participation. Not all of them will be relevant to you right now but should hopefully give you ideas for future opportunities to increase your presentation skills in your career. Pick the ones you feel comfortable with and go from there. As a rule of thumb, your job interview is not the time to test out anything new. Additionally you want to be careful not to come across as 'gimmicky' in those sorts of situations so using technology is probably not appropriate. Use your judgment when deciding what level of audience participation you'll include. The key thing is to interpret the brief for an interview scenario – what is it that they are looking for? Go back to Chapter 19 to review the skill sets that an interview panel might look for. Similarly if you are at the start of your career and just beginning to take up speaking opportunities, stick to the low-tech questions and discussion format of audience interaction and gradually work your way up from there.

Interaction before your presentation

There are several ways in which you can begin connecting with members of your audience even before you deliver your presentation. If you are speaking at a seminar that your company is organizing for example, take some time to mingle with the guests during registration. Networking in this way helps reduce nerves because you break the ice. Keep to short conversations without giving away too much about your topic. If you ask people what they hope to get from your talk or what issues they are interested in, you may be able to reference insights later either during your talk or when you deal with questions. Similarly, even if you are not in control of the event for example at an assessment centre – the entire day forms part of your assessment. People notice how you show up and the effort that you make to interact with others outside of organized activities such as group presentations or problem solving through role playing.

Another way to begin the interaction earlier is to use online surveys or polls before the event. You can email the guest list and ask them what they want covered – that way you have a great opportunity to tailor your content to the audience's needs. Even if you are delivering a presentation to your team or another department in your organization – send out a few emails or ask a couple of people directly what they would like to get out of your talk. Obviously, this isn't something you could do in an interview situation but something to think about when you do land that job and have more control over your presentation and the logistics.

Using multimedia to enrich audience experience

In my opinion anything that goes beyond simply lecturing counts as audience interaction. Participation can be at various degrees of involvement. Using music or video clips not only add variety and address the different learning styles, they engage people's emotions. Well chosen images can do this as well.

The Monkey Business Illusion video discussed in Chapter 5 is a good example of how to use video to invite audience participation. Rather than just passively watching the clip, the instructions specifically ask the viewer to actively do something – in this case to count the number of basketball passes between the teams. This is a fun short clip that generates discussion because the number of passes is not the only thing going on in this video and everyone in the room will have focused on different aspects.

You can also use these types of media to enhance your stories. Storytelling is of course the best way to connect with emotions – when you draw your audience in, they become involved in your scene – it hooks them in. Remember from Chapter 7 – people will always remember your stories long after your presentation is over.

Demonstrations and props

On 9 January 2007, Steve Jobs gave a presentation at the launch of the first iPhone to a packed auditorium in the Moscone Centre in San Francisco. This product was not just a phone – it also combined accessing the internet and the iTunes music library. To fully demonstrate the functionality of this revolutionary new device he had connected the phone to the big screen in the conference room so that the audience could see exactly what he was doing. As Steve was showing how to access Google Maps he zoomed in to find the local Starbucks coffee shop, clicked on the hyperlinked telephone number and dialled the shop. He made a joke call about ordering a huge batch of coffees for his entire audience before cancelling the order and hanging up. The barista on the other end of the line had no idea who she was speaking to and only found out afterwards! The audience, however, were in on the joke and therefore actively participating in this demonstration. They had no idea Steve was going to make the first iPhone call right there in front of their eyes and do it in such a fun way; what could have just been a product demonstration turned into a spontaneous prank. Except it wasn't. Obviously he'd planned for it in advance but the impression he gave was that it was off the cuff. This is a really good example of injecting a little bit of fun and interest into a presentation – resulting in a big laugh from the audience. Yes, the audience were still sitting in their seats watching what went on, but their level of interaction was on an emotional level. The video of this product launch is on YouTube if you want to see it for yourself.

Another simple yet equally great example is that of Bill Gates (Microsoft Founder) giving a TED talk in 2009 – *Mosquitos, Malaria and Education*. As Bill begins his talk, you notice that there is glass jar sitting on a small table to one side of him. The first part of the presentation is about the continued incidences of malaria in less developed countries. About 5 minutes into the presentation he takes the lid off the glass jar and tells the audience that he has just released mosquitos into the room. There is a nervous laugh – could Bill be joking?! After a few seconds he advises that these mosquitos are not infected – the audience can relax. For a few seconds all sorts of emotions will have been triggered in the minds of his audience. This was a shock tactic but a very effective one – why should the people living in deprived conditions thousands of miles away be the only ones to have mosquitos flying around? I highly recommend watching this video to see a good example of using a prop and injecting humour. The other great thing to look out for is the slides – they are simple and visually appealing. The photos cover the whole slide with only one tag line laid over the image and the graphs are simple and easy to follow.

The above two examples show how to use props in an unusual way and get a reaction out of the audience. You don't need to be that flamboyant. It is possible to keep it simple and still invite interaction. Using a book as your prop can still create engagement if for example you invite the audience to go away and read it or ask if anyone has come across it and if so ask for their opinion.

Incorporating questions and discussion

We've covered how to deal with questions from the audience or an interview panel in Chapter 20, when you as the speaker are put on the spot. Here we turn the tables and look at how you can be proactive and involve your audience by seeking their opinion. Invite questions.

Let's start with rhetorical questions – asking the audience something without expecting an answer. This is very low level and easy to incorporate if you don't feel confident enough to try many of the other suggestions in this chapter or the situation doesn't lend itself to increased participation. Ask rhetorical questions as you move through your presentation. An easy way to do this is to turn statements into questions. You can invite your audience to think about your argument:

- How might this affect you…?
- What would you do…?
- How can we address this problem…?
- What would happen if…?
- Would you agree that…?

A similar tactic is to invite them to visualize a situation or outcome by using the word 'imagine…'. Like posing a rhetorical question, you are not asking them to share out loud to the room the thoughts that may be going through their mind, but they are participating individually and becoming involved in your presentation.

Asking for a show of hands in response to your question is real time polling. You are getting a feel for what the audience is thinking in that moment – for example you could ask them how many agree/disagree with your point. There are pros and cons to this. Some people don't like putting their hands up and will never engage with this type of thing but at least they think about the question in their heads. On the other hand, it does help to bring people back to the present if their minds start to wander.

Taking this up a notch, you can ask people to vote by getting up from their seats. Invite people to vote with their feet by moving to one side of the room if they agree and the other side if they disagree. Then ask each group to nominate one person to explain their choice. You will of course have to think about the practicalities of this in terms of the size and layout of the room and use your common sense. If there is enough room to do this then make sure you have a plan for how you will control the room and get everyone's attention. It's quite probable that people will get carried away in their group discussions and you need to explain the ground rules before you invite them to move. See below for ideas on how to do this.

Another way to do something like this is to get people to discuss a question or issue with their neighbour for a few minutes and then you can ask them to share their views with the wider group later. This is a really easy way to get your audience to participate and is less conspicuous for those that don't like to put their hand up in front of a room full on people to answer questions. By discussing in pairs or small groups, when one person feeds back to the whole room they do so on behalf of their small group not themselves, so they feel less anxious. Group discussions add a peer learning dimension – deepening the impact through sharing experiences. Usually when people start talking in groups it can generate a buzz in the room which is fantastic because that is what you want – increasing the level of engagement. However, make sure you have a signal to alert them when time is up for the mini breakout session. If you have a large group it can get quite loud and they may not hear you when you try to get them to stop discussing. One of the tactics I use is to hold up my hand so that as soon as anyone sees that they know to stop talking and the rest of the room follows.

Usually in business presentations there is an expectation that the audience will have an opportunity to ask questions at the end of the session. As we covered in Chapter 20, tell the audience at the start how you want to tackle questions. I would encourage you to say that you'll welcome questions because you want interaction. Give them instructions as to when you will be taking questions – are you comfortable taking them at any time or will you stop at the end of each section to have a short Q and A or leave them until the end? By integrating questions throughout your presentation rather than saving them for the end turns the session into a more conversational experience. What happens when you invite questions and no one asks you anything? Well, it can actually be a brilliant opportunity to showcase your expertise. Remember in the planning phase of your presentation you will have gathered more material than you can put into your talk. You can now bring some of that extra material in to fill the void and say something like:

'A question that comes up quite often is…' or 'another example of this is…'

You might be able to share a client case study or discuss a research article. Usually this gets people thinking and they are then inspired to ask questions. Plan ahead by considering the type of audience you have and think about typical questions they might want to ask and then prepare for them so that you are ready. Think about what you will say or do if you don't get the reaction or response you want.

When you do invite questions, allow time for a response and acknowledge contributions politely – when you make people feel that their opinions matter, they are more likely to be engaged. Make sure you listen and if necessary ask if they can repeat the question again so that you are clear and that the rest of the audience can hear it as well so that they can be involved. Once you have shared your personal thoughts think about opening the question up to the rest of the room – ask if anyone has any further thoughts on the matter. By doing that you can generate a discussion. For more tips on dealing with questions go back over to Chapter 20.

Quizzes to enhance your presentation

Gamification has become very popular in the training and development industry at the moment, particularly in respect of e-learning. This approach makes training more meaningful as delegates are better engaged. Human beings have a natural desire for achievement and competition – if you've got the latest trendy games on your smartphone or are surrounded by people that do, then you'll know what I'm talking about. Similarly, in the workplace, through the use of healthy competition within the training modules, employees are more incentivized to learn. Including games as team building activities at corporate away days is also quite common. So how is this relevant to your presentation? Instead of just broadcasting your material, allow your participants to actively engage with the information by incorporating some content into a quiz. When I say quiz, I don't mean you necessarily have to design a whole segment. You can just ask your audience to guess fun facts at the end of each section perhaps. Or you might use a case study or recap of what you have covered as the basis of your quiz. Tell them that you will be asking them questions to see if they remember key facts at the end of your presentation – it might make them concentrate more.

In Chapter 10 I shared a case study where the presenter asked the audience to guess how many litres it would take to fill an Olympic swimming pool. He did this in a very simple way by putting a picture of a pool on a slide and then asking the audience to shout out answers to his question. It was fun and broke the ice because he used this tactic right at the beginning of his team talk. When he revealed the correct answer he tied it into how that fun fact related to the topic of the presentation.

To make this more visual, use your slides to help you. Rather than simply telling the audience a fact ask them to guess from multiple choice or true/false options that you display on the screen. Then tie it into your key point.

Using software to support audience interaction

This final section is perhaps not as relevant for you now especially if you are in the early stages of your career, preparing for an interview or assessment centre. However, I think you'll find it useful by way of background should you ever have to prepare for speaking to bigger audiences at conferences or are part of a team hosting such events.

I've talked about using your slides to ask quiz type questions – very easy to construct as well as being visual. There are actually many sophisticated software applications available to help you do this as well. Some are free to use and others are subscription based. There are specific event apps with Q and A functionality that provide the option of asking anonymous questions. Many people are hesitant to ask questions in front of others for fear of looking silly. Of course you don't have to keep it anonymous though if you want to collect specific data but at least the audience member has the choice as whether they share their name. Some of the options I've come across so far are Glisser, Sli.do and Poll Everywhere but there are many others. Most of these work on the basis that individuals can download an app to their mobile device and you create an event code which people can join.

They are then able to ask questions in real time – anyone signed up to the event can see all the questions being posed which makes it more inclusive. The presenter can scan them and choose when and which ones to answer. You can also ask people to vote for the correct answer to a quiz type question or conduct polls. The results are instantly displayed within your slide deck on the screen for everyone to see. People enjoy polls because they can share their opinion as well as see how they compare to everyone else. Another benefit offered by these apps is the ability to leverage social media for example by creating an event hashtag for twitter so that people can share insights from your talk and connect/network with each other.

Sometimes wireless internet access is not available or the connection is not good enough to successfully use these types of mobile apps. You can use voting pads instead. They work in a similar way to the apps for answering questions where you give people a choice of answers. The disadvantage is that you can't type questions, the audience can only vote from a choice of answers or options. On the plus side they work without internet access on a radio frequency, allow people to answer anonymously and introduce an element of fun.

Conclusion

In this chapter I've given you ideas about different ways in which to incorporate audience interaction from low tech questions for the audience to high tech polling and quizzes using slides, apps and smartphones. Some of these ideas are more appropriate for conference type events or client seminars and not relevant for interview situations as mentioned above. They are all great in different situations. When you are just getting started with delivering presentations, start small with something like asking your audience to discuss a question in pairs and then as your expertise grows move onto fun quizzes using slides and apps.

TOP TIPS

- Get the audience to do something – this will help them commit new material to memory.

- Take some key points from your presentation and turn them into a quiz type question for more participation

- Have at least one or two instances built into your talk where you either ask a rhetorical question or ask the audience to answer – it forces them to engage and think which increases knowledge retention

- Research software tools for audience engagement even if you don't need to use them in your current role, to get you thinking about trends and innovative ways to interact with your audience

CONCLUSION

When it comes to mastering presentation technique, the path to improvement never ends – there is always more room to refine. Even the most experienced speakers want to keep improving and dedicate their efforts towards that. Speakers don't suddenly become great overnight – they go through a process of development over time. What do you want to do with your presentations and speaking opportunities? How will they slot into your career path?

Now that you've worked through the steps in this book you might want to have a look back through the chapters and review the tops tips for a quick refresher. The top tips are deliberately placed as a quick summary at the end of each chapter for easy reference.

If you initially picked up this book in preparation for an interview or your first professional presentation in front of an audience, think about how you can now enhance your skills and develop your speaking style. For additional practice, you could try joining a speaking club such as Toastmasters International or if you are up for a slightly different kind of challenge – how about taking a stand-up comedy class? I learnt a lot about writing and delivering punchy and entertaining anecdotes from the course I took. If you want to get more comfortable at fielding difficult questions then what better place to test your nerve than in front of a heckling crowd when you do your 5 minute set at an open mic night after you've completed the course?!

Choose one or two chapters to work with again and take a deep dive to concentrate on improving individual areas. Perhaps start off with having a look back through Chapters 7 and 21 which cover presentation styles – in particular storytelling, and audience interaction. Storytelling is one of the best techniques for connecting with your audience – developing a bank of stories and honing them so that they become easy to recount whenever you want takes time but is absolutely worth the effort. How will you start to build your own file of stories and anecdotes? Connecting with your audience through compelling storytelling is a key component of successful presentations but you also want to think about how to improve audience interaction. For longer speech slots or more senior audience members you have to find ways to keep their attention – drawing them into interesting discussions is a good starting point. You might want to incorporate technology and use polls through apps if it's a conference type event. Experiment with introducing one of these ideas each time you are presenting.

Whether you are just getting started or already have quite a bit of speaking experience, remember that you want to make the information you share with your audience as accessible and memorable as possible. The best way to do this is by putting that information into context. Remember the Olympic pool and Steve Jobs examples in Chapter 7? Practice finding ways to hook your messages next to every day examples or things that people are already familiar with so that they understand your meaning in their own way.

On a final note, every time you prepare for a presentation always test and adapt – build in enough time to rehearse and get feedback either from others or recording on your smartphone. You want to see and hear what the audience will experience because after all, the presentation is for them. Keep videos of your talks or rehearsal so you have reference points and can track your improvements.

Here's to your sparkling speaking success.

INDEX

Page numbers in *italic* indicate Figures.